From the Pigpen
to the Pulpit

From the Pigpen to the Pulpit
by Pastor Bill Sammons

Copyright © 2009 William T. Sammons
ISBN 978-1-886068-35-3
Christian Life · Religious and Inspirational · Personal Growth · Faith
Library of Congress Control Number
2009925265

Published by Fruitbearer Publishing, L.L.C.
P.O. Box 777, Georgetown, DE 19947
(302) 856-6649 · FAX (302) 856-7742
www.fruitbearer.com • info@fruitbearer.com

Edited by Fran D. Lowe
Cover Illustration by Josh Sammons

Unless otherwise noted, Scripture is taken from *The New King James Version (NKJV)*. Copyright © 1982 by Thomas Nelson, Inc. Used by permission. All rights reserved.

Scripture quotations marked (NIV) are taken from the *NEW INTERNATIONAL VERSION®, NIV®*. Copyright © 1973, 1978, 1984 International Bible Society. Used by permission of Zondervan Bible Publishers. All rights reserved.

Scripture quotations marked (NLT) are taken from the *Holy Bible, New Living Translation,* copyright © 1996. Used by permission of Tyndale House Publishers, Inc., Wheaton, IL 60189 USA. All rights reserved.

All rights reserved. No part of this publication may be reproduced, stored in a retrieval system, or transmitted in any form or by any means—electronic, mechanical, photocopy, recording, or any other—except for brief quotations in printed reviews, without the prior permission of the publisher or author, except as provided by USA copyright law.

Printed in the United States of America

FROM THE PIGPEN TO THE PULPIT

THE LIFE STORY OF ~~FARMER~~ *Pastor* BILL SAMMONS, SR.

. . . Also, I heard the voice of the Lord, saying,
"Whom shall I send and who will go for Us?"
Then said I, "Here am I, send me."
And He said, "Go" . . .
(Isaiah 6:8-9a, NIV)

DEDICATION

*This book is dedicated to my brother in Christ
and my good friend,
Hall D. "Sonny" Reed Jr.,
who has known me since we were
childhood friends in grade school.*

*Sonny has loved me,
encouraged me,
and consistently believed in me—
sometimes when I didn't believe in myself.
His life, his words, and his friendship
have influenced my life,
especially after he became the church administrator
at Eagle's Nest Fellowship Church.
What a joy to work with a man who never sees a problem,
only opportunities for God to work.*

Thank you, Sonny, for your friendship.

TABLE OF CONTENTS

Isaiah 6:8-9 v
Dedication vii
Acknowledgments xi
Introduction xiii
Who Will Go For Me? xv
Acts 29 xix

Chapter 1. My Beginning 21
Chapter 2. It's in the Book! 25
Chapter 3. A Surrendered Life 29
Chapter 4. The Journey 33
Chapter 5. Teenagers in the House 37
Chapter 6. Bible Study 39
Chapter 7. Status Offenders 41
Chapter 8. God, It's Yours 43
Chapter 9. Come Apart and Learn of Me 47
Chapter 10. Just Filling In? 49
Chapter 11. Where To Go? 51
Chapter 12. Rhema It Is! 53
Chapter 13. Foot-Washing 55
Chapter 14. Westward Bound 57
Chapter 15. Confirmation . . . Again 59
Chapter 16. 1 Kings 17 61
Chapter 17. The Spoken Word 63
Chapter 18. Being Where God Wants You 65
Chapter 19. The School Year 69
Chapter 20. The Call to Ministry 79

Chapter 21.	Reflections from the Farm	81
Chapter 22.	Fleshing Out the Call	87
Chapter 23.	Earl's Song	91
Chapter 24.	Keep Prayin'	97
Chapter 25.	You Will Only Keep What You Obey	103
Chapter 26.	What Are You Hearing?	107
Chapter 27.	The Birth of Eagle's Nest Fellowship	109
Chapter 28.	A Consensus	117
Chapter 29.	God Wants to Use People	119
Chapter 30.	God's Favor	121
Chapter 31.	Seeker-Sensitive	127
Chapter 32.	John	131
Chapter 33.	Stewards	133
Chapter 34.	Missions	137
Chapter 35.	Small-Group Ministry	139
Chapter 36.	Making Disciples	141
Chapter 37.	Messiah's Vineyard	143
Chapter 38.	Transferring the Mantle	147
Chapter 39.	The Vision Continues	149
Chapter 40.	Called by God	151
Chapter 41.	Prayer Warriors	153
Chapter 42.	Through the Shadow	155
Chapter 43.	A Higher Dimension	157
Chapter 44.	What Is Your Identity?	159
Chapter 45.	True Success	163
Chapter 46.	Called into Ministry	167
Chapter 47.	The Key	169
Chapter 48.	Teachable and Available	171
Chapter 49.	Excuses	173
Chapter 50.	Christian Education	181

About the Author	187
Order the Book	189

ACKNOWLEDGMENTS

When God calls us from The Pigpen (where we are) to The Pulpit (where He wants us to be), and we respond by saying, "Here I am Lord, send me," it affects more lives than just the one who made the decision to go.

My journey and this book could not have happened without the love and support of my family, all of whom have given their loving support to make it possible.

I am especially grateful to my loving wife of fifty-two years, Mary Jane. Never has Mary Jane been negative about anything I felt God was leading me to do. Instead, she provided encouragement and support. Even in the years before we were both serving God, she was always alongside me one hundred percent. It is a real test of a relationship when one spouse says, "I'm going to leave my job and go to school," knowing all income will stop. While I was in Tulsa, Mary Jane stayed in Delaware to work and support us.

The Bible is correct. When a man finds a wife, he has found a good thing (Prov. 18:22).

I also believe the second part of that verse. A good wife enables us to find favor. That sure has been true in my life. Thank you, Mary Jane. I love and appreciate you more than you know, and more than I did fifty-two years ago.

To our son, Bill Jr., in whom we are well pleased, I thank you for all the hours of work, reading, proofing, editing, and challenging me, as well as encouraging me in this effort. You have made it happen. Thank you.

A special thanks to our daughter-in-love, Bonny, for all the hours of checking spelling and punctuation and breaking my story into chapters. We love you very much.

To our grandsons, Josh and Nick, who make our hearts glad, thanks for your work and contributions. Nick took the photos for the cover, and Josh did the cover design and layout. This was truly a family effort.

Thank you all for living the journey with me and making this account possible.

To God be the glory!

INTRODUCTION

The purpose of this book is twofold. First, the supernatural events surrounding the vision, birth, and life of Eagle's Nest Fellowship Church need to be recorded so that future generations will be aware of the miracles that made all this possible. God's hand has been on this from the beginning. I think this is how God builds the church; I surely know that I did not build it. I have tried to remain leadable, teachable, and obedient to what I believe God was, and is, saying to me. To God be all the glory!

The second reason for this book is contained within its title. This title came from a precious saint of God, Marge Camenisch, who has loved me and prayed for me and this ministry for years. She shared with me that, while in prayer, she believed God told her what I should call this book—hence the title, *From the Pigpen to the Pulpit*. Prior to becoming a Bible teacher and a pastor, I spent many years as a hog farmer. So, this is a definitive title for the book.

I believe this title also describes so many Christians who are either comfortable where they are or concerned that they are not able or qualified to do much for God. The pigpen does not represent a place of disgust or punishment; it just represents where you are in your life and your walk with God. It clearly shows that you can get comfortable in any environment and therefore become complacent. The pigpen is where I was, but it was clearly not where God wanted me to be. This is a record of my journey from the pigpen to the pulpit.

WHO WILL GO FOR ME?

*A*s I began to write this book, I am reminded of a message I preached years ago entitled, "Chicken Christian or Eagle Christian?" In that message I preached from Deuteronomy 32:11 which states, "As an eagle stirs up its nest, hovers over its young, spreading out its wings, taking them up, carrying them on its wings . . ."

There comes a time in an eagle's life when he needs to leave the comfort of the nest. He doesn't want to go because it is very comfortable there and all his needs are met, but Momma knows best. In due season, she begins to tear up the nest and make things uncomfortable for the baby eaglet. She wants him out of the nest. It is in his best interest to go, but in order to get him out she has to make the nest uncomfortable—so uncomfortable that he hops on Momma's back to keep the sticks and barbs from hurting him any longer. The mother takes off and flies. Just when he thinks he is comfortable again on Momma's back, she dumps him off so he can learn to fly on his own.

At this point baby eagles must learn to fly, or they will die. God does the same for us by tearing up our comfy little nest, making it uncomfortable. If we don't learn to fly, the enemy of our souls will destroy us. Many of you think that what you are facing in your lives right now is the Devil because your comfort zone is being disrupted. For most of us, it is God saying, "Get out of the nest! Begin to fly and soar above the circumstances of your lives, and get involved in Kingdom living."

It was Christmas 2005 when Eagle's Nest Christian Academy administrator, Lucy Dutton, asked me about serving an appreciation dinner to all the employees of the school and daycare. We included the employees of Eagle's Nest Fellowship Church and Eagle's Nest Family Campground, and the reality set in that our ministry now had almost a hundred full-time employees.

I think that was the first time it really dawned on me all that God had done in fourteen short years. As I reflected on the number of employees, I thought about how it all started and how God could use even me to birth three churches collectively ministering to about sixteen hundred people weekly; a Christian pre K-8 school with over four hundred students; a Christian-operated daycare for a hundred children; and Eagle's Nest Family Campground, a family-focused setting based on Isaiah 40:31 where families can find rest and renewal for their spirits, souls, and bodies in a relaxed atmosphere.

The following chapters give an account of how God ruffled my nest. He taught me to fly above my own abilities by trusting Him and all the people He has sent me to birth a series of ministries.

I want to be quite clear about God's role in all of this. I am convinced—and am living proof—that God will use any vessel committed to Him. God always seems to use the ones who are willing and then qualifies them, rather than trying to make the qualified ones willing.

The prophet Isaiah is an example of this. Isaiah 6 relates the events of his conversion. Nowhere in that story does God choose Isaiah. The process goes like this: Young Isaiah is in the temple, probably worshiping, and he sees God. After he sees God, he sees himself. When he sees himself, he doesn't like himself; so he cries out, "Woe is me, for I am undone!" Only when we see God do we feel inadequate about ourselves. There must be a crying out to God before He will move to send someone to heal our unclean lips, which represents whatever our need is. After Isaiah encounters God and is cleansed by Him, He asks the question, "Who will go for Me?" Isaiah responds, "Here am I, send me" (Isaiah 6:1-8).

I love this story because it is so similar to mine. I am writing this because I am convinced that there are many Isaiah's in our churches who will never go because they don't feel qualified or they are waiting for God to write it in the sky. In reality, however, God is saying to all of us in some capacity, "Who will go for Me?"

If you remember anything from this book, let it be this: Don't wait until you are perfect. If God has saved you, He will do things in you and through you that you never dreamed possible, but you will never walk on water unless you get out of the boat.

ACTS 29

*T*ake a minute right now and read Acts 29, keeping in mind that if God can use me, He can use you. (Remember, He used a donkey one time!)

Did you read it? If you tried to read Chapter 29 of the Book of Acts, you know it's not there! I am convinced, however, that there is a Chapter 29, and we are it.

The Book of Acts is a record of how God continues to work in and through the church, not just in and through the Lord Jesus Christ. In fact, Luke, who wrote the Gospel of Luke as well as Acts, dedicates both books to Theophilus. We are not sure who he is, but we know that his name means "beloved of God." Luke begins Acts by reminding this "beloved of God" of all that Jesus did in His three years of ministry as He was filled with and empowered by the Holy Spirit. Read about His baptism in Luke 3:21-22.

In Acts, Luke is sharing all about what God did in and through Jesus, who was empowered by the Holy Spirit. He shares what is continuing to happen by the Holy Spirit through the church. This Holy Spirit is no longer confined to one person, Jesus, because the sin debt has been paid. Pentecost has come in a new and living way. The Holy Spirit will empower as many as are willing to receive Him (Acts 2:1-4).

The baptism of the Holy Spirit is not optional but essential for the church and commanded by Jesus before we begin any ministry. Don't get caught up in debates about how or when, or what gifts to expect; just decide you want the fullness of His Spirit operating in your life. After Peter's sermon in Acts 2, three thousand more were added to the church. Thus, the promise is for all of us, not just some select few (Acts 2:39).

After Peter and John prayed for the man who couldn't walk in Acts 3, five thousand more were added to the church. All of this is a result of the empowering of the Holy Spirit and the disciples' receptiveness to what God desired to do through them. This is why it's important to see that Acts 29 is being written by us. How are you doing with your verses?

How do you begin? What is the first step in this journey from "the pigpen to the pulpit"? I think that for most of us, we—like Paul—must "forget those things that are behind." Don't let your past hinder, or even steal, your future. God has forgiven you if you have asked Him. Now forgive yourself.

What are the influences in our lives that shape us? I am confident that all the events of our lives shape us. I am also convinced that every circumstance of our lives will make us either bitter or better. None of those experiences will leave us the same. The circumstances of our lives are not what is important, but what we do with them.

CHAPTER 1

MY BEGINNING

I was raised in a good home, even though it was not a Christian home. My father passed away at the age of forty-nine from a heart attack, but not before he instilled in me a work ethic that "anything you do is worth doing well." I was only seventeen when he died. Many decades later, I had the joy of praying with my mother to accept Christ when she was in her eighties. Both Mom's tender heart and Dad's hard work ethic greatly affected me. At any rate, college or any higher education was never a topic of discussion in our home. Dad and Mom's eighth-grade education influenced them to believe that just getting my two brothers and me through high school was a lofty enough goal.

Though there was an absence of spiritual influence in our home, I knew that Mom and Dad believed that there was a God. My first spiritual event happened when I was eight or nine years old. Mom and Dad had decided that my older brother and I should be baptized. They arranged for neighbors to pick up my brother and me and take us to church to be baptized during the morning service. I was old enough to be scared out of my wits but not old enough to understand what was happening. Before I could be sprinkled, the pastor said I had to be saved, yet I did not understand. Saved from what?

At the altar, there was much crying and laughing, as well as displays of emotion with loud shouts that had a negative impact on me. It frightened me so badly that I didn't ever go back to that church again. No one had explained anything to me. They just forced me to go to the altar, and I didn't understand what was happening.

Years later, I visited a Pentecostal church with Mary Jane, my fiancée. Some of her family attended there and had begged us to go. We finally said yes and attended a Sunday night service.

While there, all those childhood memories came rushing back. I was sure that if this was God, I did not want or need Him. I think it's important to mention here that I don't ever remember a time in my life when I didn't believe there was a God. I always believed there was a God, yet I felt that this Pentecostal experience was not God. Little did I know there really was a Pentecost, and it was very real.

When we got married, Mary Jane was the secretary of the Sunday school department at Goshen United Methodist Church in Milton, Delaware. She faithfully attended church, and I went to the services sometimes. (After all, I didn't want to be a fanatic.)

After our son, Bill Jr., was born, Mary Jane saw to it that he had perfect attendance in church from the time he was one until he was in his teens. In 1972, when Bill Jr. was fifteen years old, we moved to a small farm near Ellendale, Delaware, which required a change of school districts. After transferring to Milford High School, he made some new friends who attended a church that was sponsoring a trip to Dallas, Texas, to attend Explo '72. Described by *Newsweek* magazine at the time, Explo '72 was a "Christian Woodstock" sponsored by Campus Crusade for Christ, an organization founded by Bill Bright. I had no idea that our lives would never be the same again, after Bill's trip to Dallas.

After returning from Texas, I asked our son what had impressed him most at Explo '72, thinking he would talk about seeing Roger Staubach or hearing and meeting André Crouch, the famed gospel singer. I was taken aback when he replied that his greatest experience was being born again—giving his heart to Jesus. I wasn't prepared for that.

He asked me if I was saved, and I replied, "From what?" I really thought that this was some teenage fad that would pass, yet it did not. I could argue with my son's words but not the change I saw in him. Now, he stopped hanging around some old friends and began to make new ones. He also really desired to go to church and its events.

The following year our Methodist church sponsored a Lay Witness Mission, and our son was very excited about it. A Lay Witness Mission is a weekend event during which laypeople from out of town share their testimonies of how they became Christians and the ways Jesus is working in their lives. We housed one of the youth members of the team and had to be involved in the events because of the distance we lived from the church. (It made sense to stay and participate rather than just be a chauffeur for them.) So, like it or not, I was involved in a Lay Witness Mission.

Having never met people like this in my life, I was convinced they were phonies. They talked about Jesus like He was their best friend and acted as if they had just had lunch with Him. I saw men hugging men—something that really scared me. I was sure they were not real and told God so on Sunday morning when Mary Jane and I went to the altar to pray after the morning message. My heart was sincere and my head messed up as I prayed, "Lord, if this is real, then do it in me, because I don't know You like that, Amen."

There was no thunder or lightning: nothing. No one even came to pray with me. I just returned to my pew.

God has a way of honoring our heart's cry, and He almost immediately began a new work in me. Prior to the Lay Witness Mission, I had been teaching a Sunday school class of young married couples. Can you imagine? I was unsaved but still teaching others!

After my altar experience on Sunday morning, which was the first time I recall kneeling at an altar other than during communion, it was as though someone had messed with my Bible. As I began to prepare for my next class, the passages somehow read differently. The best way I know how to describe it is that the Bible changed from being a history book to a Book of Life for me. I saw Jesus everywhere, and I also saw myself and began to cry out for help (Isaiah 6). Because of this event, the Bible is very important to me. I began to have a hunger for the Word that has never left to this day.

IT'S IN THE BOOK!

Several years later at a meeting in Salisbury, Maryland, I had the pleasure of hearing Harold Hill speak. Harold had been an agnostic when he started working with our nation's space program in its earliest days. Through his research, he became convinced that there had to be an Intelligence behind creation as he observed the exact logic within the universe. He decided to call this Intelligence "God." He then began a search to know this God and became a committed, born-again Christian. He later wrote the best-selling book entitled From Goo to You by Way of the Zoo, which disputes the theory of evolution.

That night in Maryland, Harold Hill used a phrase that I had never heard before—one that would have a deep impact on my life. Harold called the Bible the "Manufacturer's Handbook."

What a marvelous description of this book! Most of us have had the frustration of putting something together that is in many pieces, and we still think we know how to do it. Without reading the manufacturer's handbook, however, we miss key steps and end up frustrated. When all else fails, then we read the book.

I once had a teacher in high school who taught a course called "Problems of Democracy." When our class could not answer a question concerning our homework assignment, Mrs. (Esther) Weakley would slam the book down on her desk and yell, "It's in the book!"

I am sure God has probably felt that way many times with me, exclaiming, "It's in the Book!" The Bible tells us how to live life abundantly. It teaches us how to be a better wife, husband, mother, father, employee, employer, and even citizen of this kingdom as well as the Kingdom of God.

I live in a rural community where farming is a way of life. It is not uncommon for a farmer to pay $250,000 and up for a piece of equipment. When you pay that much money for machinery, you really need to know how to operate it efficiently. Most read the manufacturer's handbook so they can have as many trouble-free hours as possible. We are much more valuable than that $250,000 amount, but we don't seem to have the desire to read the handbook written by the One who made us. It tells us how to live life to the fullest, with as few breakdowns as possible. Jesus said in John 10:10, "I have come that they may have life, and that they may have it more abundantly."

Abundant life comes when we acknowledge that the One who made us knows more about us than we know about ourselves. He knows what will fulfill us and make us happy. We receive this abundant living by not doing what we want, but what He wants. Freedom does not mean we can do whatever we want.

Earl Tyson, my spiritual father whom I will say more about later, shared a story about kite-flying one night in a revival service. I don't know if it was original with him or not, but it's a great analogy. Earl said if the kite could talk, it would probably say to the string, "Let me go, you are holding me back. If you would just let go so I have no restraints, I could soar much higher and further." The truth is, however, that the string is what enables the kite to fly. If the string breaks, the kite crashes.

So it is with us. We must let God constrain us, or we crash. Let me urge you to READ THE BOOK! We will soar as high as God allows us when we live our lives surrendered to Him. I don't know how to succeed in life without surrendering to God as He has revealed Himself in Jesus. We all have to surrender and resign as general managers of ourselves, get off the throne of our lives, and make Him not only Savior but Lord. That means He is now our Boss.

A SURRENDERED LIFE

*F*or fear of sounding prideful or self-edifying, I have written this chapter with reluctance. I know that what has happened in my life is the result of God working in and through me while I have sought to be led by Him. There is nothing in me that has enabled me to succeed. In fact, I'm not sure I know what success really is, but I do know that true failure is to live one's life ignoring God. Because He loves us, He has a plan and purpose for us. He has designed a place for us so that we may help fulfill His ultimate plan and purpose for our lives.

I know that mere human wisdom, education, or tradition will not enable us to bear much fruit in the Kingdom of God. We must live our lives filled with and empowered by the Holy Spirit. Jesus didn't begin His ministry until His water baptism when the Holy Spirit came upon Him and remained (Luke 3 and 4). Chapter 4 of Luke's gospel begins with this telling statement, "Jesus, being filled with the Holy Spirit, was led by the Spirit into the wilderness where He was tempted forty days by the devil."

Notice that after Jesus overcame all the temptations, He came out of that experience armed with the power of the Holy Spirit. It is important to note the sequence: He was filled with the Holy Spirit at His water baptism; He was then led by the Holy Spirit into the wilderness, where He was tempted for forty days. After overcoming the tempter, Jesus came out of the wilderness armed with the power of the Holy Spirit.

It is not enough to be filled with the Holy Spirit—or even led by the Spirit. We must be armed with the power of the Spirit to do ministry as Jesus did. This is what Jesus wanted for the disciples, and He wants it for us as well. After His crucifixion and resurrection, He commanded His disciples before His ascension not to begin any ministry until they had received power from the Holy Spirit (Acts 1:4-8). For too long, the church has tried to minister without the power of Pentecost. It is not optional!

Pentecost is not just an Old Testament feast day, nor is it just a New Testament date to celebrate the birth of the church. Although Pentecost is both of those, it is so much more. The church was birthed by the one hundred and twenty people who experienced the Person of the Holy Spirit in an empowering way. Likewise, every believer needs to experience their own personal Pentecost to be equipped for ministry.

When God called me into full-time ministry in the early eighties, I was raising pigs. Even though I was in my forties with only a high school diploma and very little money, I was happy. But

I knew that God was directing me to leave the farm and attend Bible college in Tulsa, Oklahoma. Thankfully at that time, I did not know all that God had in store for me. I probably would have been overwhelmed and run the other way!

If you had told me back then that one day I'd be involved in establishing several churches, a daycare, a school, a campground, and more, I would have not believed that it was possible. Yet, He took my willing heart, sent me people with gifts that I did not possess, and allowed me to see a vision come to reality.

I don't want to minimize the fact that God surrounded me with people who were key to everything that has been accomplished in the past twenty-five years. It is not possible to mention everyone's name in this book; but if you are (or have been) a volunteer or employee in any of the Eagle's Nest ministries, you have been a vital part of what makes them successful, and I thank God for you!

THE JOURNEY

Billy Graham Association Crusade

After our Lay Witness Mission, I could not quench the hunger in my soul for the Word of God. The following year, our small state of Delaware experienced the joy of sponsoring a Billy Graham Association Crusade at the State Fairgrounds in Harrington. John Wesley White was the evangelist for the event.

I was a brand-new Christian, but Mary Jane convinced me that we should take the Life and Witness Classes, which would prepare us and the army of volunteers to be used during the crusade itself. These classes were required for all volunteer workers participating in the crusade, not only the altar workers, but everyone from the choir to the follow-up team processing all the commitment cards that would be turned in. The classes were held to ensure that all the volunteers knew that they were saved and could share their faith effectively. Taking those excellent classes was vital to my spiritual growth because they removed all of my fear that I might not be saved. For the first time, I realized that my salvation depended on what Jesus had already done—not on my own goodness.

These classes were so timely at this point in my walk with God. Before the Billy Graham Crusade, whenever I heard a good salvation sermon, I wanted to get saved all over again. After attending the classes, I found myself praying for others instead of just myself.

The next major event in my journey involved a week of services at our Methodist church that was led by Earl Tyson, an approved conference evangelist from the Virginia Conference. Earl's ministry had a very special impact on me, my family, our church, and community. I saw in him the fruit of ministry that is channeled with love and compassion for all.

During the last night of services at our church, he gave an invitation to those who wanted to receive the fullness of the Holy Spirit in their lives. Mary Jane and I were hungering for more so we went forward to the altar for prayer. Six-foot-five Earl laid his baseball glove-sized hands on us and began to pray. Heaven opened up! We began to laugh, cry, pray, and rejoice. It was like taking a bath inside and out at the same time; we truly experienced a tremendous cleansing and a peace that was supernatural. After this supernatural cleansing, we tried to rise from the altar, but the process would start all over again. I thought we had been there perhaps around twenty minutes; yet when we finally rose from the altar, we discovered it had been an hour and a half. The church was empty except for Earl and our pastor, and most of the lights had been turned off.

For the first time in my life, I felt like a pure vessel. I was at peace with God, myself, and all those around me. I now understood how the renowned Methodist missionary E. Stanley Jones felt after his conversion in Baltimore when he remarked, "I just wanted to wrap my arms around the world and love them for Jesus."

This event marked the beginning of my life in the Spirit. This involved many aspects of my life; but most importantly, I discovered that God did indeed have a plan, purpose, and a place for my life. All my life I had just gone where the wind blew me. I had no goals, no direction, and no desires—except to survive. Now it seemed as though God was interested in my life. What a surprise! God wanted to use me? That God could use me was as much of a surprise as anything.

CHAPTER 5

TEENAGERS IN THE HOUSE

Just as my Bible was apparently tampered with, so was my affinity toward teenagers. Suddenly, I liked them! God seemed to be leading my wife and me to become leaders of the youth group at our Methodist church. With much fear and trembling on my part, we began.

Because our son was a teen, we basically started with his friends, but we also met some hungry teens who had been deeply touched by God at the Lay Witness Mission. They needed someone to mentor and teach them, as well as love them into wholeness. God blessed the ministry, and the numbers grew to about forty-five active members in our group.

Weekends at our farmhouse near Ellendale became a gathering place for teens to play ball games, swim in the pool, or just hang out with dozens of other youth. We learned that many of our teens could sing, so our youth group soon began singing at area churches, nursing homes, and public events.

At least three people from this group later entered into full-time ministry. John Betts became the senior pastor of Abundant Life Church in Georgetown, Delaware; his brother, Rick Betts, who served as worship leader and associate pastor for ten years at Eagle's Nest Fellowship Church, became the pastor of Crossroads Community Church near Bridgeville, Delaware, (one of the churches that grew out of Eagle's Nest); and our son, Bill Jr., started the first Christian radio station in Delaware, WXPZ 101.3 FM, out of Milford.

CHAPTER 6

BIBLE STUDY

One of the other major changes in our lives after Earl's revival services involved beginning a Bible study in our home every Thursday night. We would have forty to fifty people show up, some of whom we did not even know. This was during the middle to late seventies, when it seemed as if you said the name "Jesus," someone would get saved! There definitely was a revival going on in America, and we were immersed in the middle of it in southern Delaware.

This Thursday night group began after I announced to our Sunday school class that we needed someone to lead the study. John and Jane Phillips, who had been teachers at our Methodist church for some time, agreed to lead the group and God did the rest!

John and Jane made a very big impact on my life. Both were solid, Bible-believing, principled, moral Christians who loved people. John passed from this life on to glory before Eagle's Nest

Fellowship Church began. Jane became an active member and prayer warrior at Eagle's Nest Fellowship Church before joining her beloved husband in heaven in 2007.

STATUS OFFENDERS

Our involvement with the youth of the Methodist church led us to want to do more for all the troubled youth with whom we came in contact. Our call from God led us to a program the State of Delaware was starting for troubled teens which they called "Status Offenders."

These were teens who had not been criminally charged but were in trouble at home or with the authorities. Often it was the result of parents declaring them uncontrollable, or in most cases, runaways. Prior to the opening of our home to them, all runaways were taken to the Stevenson House in Milford, Delaware, by the police. The Stevenson House is an incarceration facility for teens charged with serious crimes. Runaways were housed with teens who had violent histories, drug problems, or worse. Obviously this wasn't a good mix because the status offenders were often just experiencing problems at home and did not have criminal records.

This time of our lives brought about many changes. In order to house more teens, we put our small farm up for sale, and God provided us with a nine-bedroom home located on five acres near Milford for this ministry.

It was a rude awakening to discover that not all of these teens responded to our love and concern. When the first one ran away from us, I couldn't believe it! Why would anyone run away from us? We had a beautiful home filled with love and nurturing, warm beds, plenty of food, and family. Mary Jane's mother moved in and became "Mom Mom" to every child who came. Mary Jane's sister, Doris, moved in to cook meals. (Boy, could she cook!) We found an antique dining room table that could seat about sixteen people, so dinner time often looked like a scene from "The Waltons."

Yet, we still had some runaways. Over the years we had forty-nine teens living in our home. During this time we discovered that just loving them was not enough to reverse the damage of many years of poor parenting. I never had a child living with us who surprised me, but I sure met a lot of parents who disappointed me.

In one case we saw a year of progress disappear after one weekend at the teen's home, where drugs were readily available. If I had not seen this, I would not have believed it. It was during this time that God gave us a burden for families, beginning with marriages. The daycare, Christian school, and even church cannot effect change in children if it's not being reinforced in the home. God designed the institution of marriage before the church, school, or daycare. We must first heal the homes of our world—one at a time—as people encounter the living God, whose name is Jesus.

GOD, IT'S YOURS

One day, one of our teens decided to smoke a cigarette in the one-hundred-year-old barn, situated just across the horseshoe driveway that wrapped around the house. He carelessly flipped the butt out on the roof and set the barn on fire. It was a beautiful two-and-a-half story barn made of mostly white oak lumber. Boy, did it burn! By the time the fire department arrived, the concern was not the barn because it was too late to save it.

The danger now was that the house could also burn. Before the fire department came, flaming debris from the barn was starting to fall on the roof of the house. Ronnie and Donna Mitchell, our neighbors and best friends as well as back-up Dad and Mom for the teens, had arrived on the scene. The winds were blowing probably twenty to thirty miles per hour and were directly aimed at the house. Ronnie and I were fighting a losing battle, armed with just a garden hose. Panic was setting in on me because I was sure we would lose the house too.

As I tried in vain to extinguish the flames, I felt it was my duty to remind God of all of our financial sacrifices to make this home and ministry possible. I warned Him that if He did not change the wind, it would all go up in smoke; but nothing changed.

Finally in total surrender, I said, "Lord, this is Your house and Your ministry. If You want it to burn down, it's okay with me." With that confession, I threw down the puny, little garden hose on the roof. As soon as the hose hit the roof, the wind changed and started blowing away from the house. Later, as I was testifying to the fire department about the miracle, the chief said that a fire of that magnitude would create its own wind, so that was probably why it changed direction. I replied that it may be so, but you could visibly see that this fire had made two ninety-degree turns around the house as it had burned green soybean fields in two directions, ultimately sparing our home and ministry.

While I was attending Bible school over a year later, God showed me an important principle using that prayer. I believe that God was prompted to move only after I released our home and ministry to Him. My earlier prayer of "God, if You don't do something, Your house and Your ministry will burn" had been offered in fear. The latter prayer, "God, it's Yours," was prayed in surrender and faith. I really did feel peace after I uttered the second prayer. Hebrews 11:6 tells us that it takes faith to please God. The Bible also tells us that God has not given us a spirit of fear (2 Timothy 1:7). I believe fear paralyzes us and hinders God.

During this time in our journey, God was continuing to increase our burden for marriages. I am not a marriage counselor, but God has used me to bring healing in many marriages. Let me ask you a question: Do you think divorce played a part in those status-offending teens' lives? Now let me give you a statistic.

Of the forty-nine teens who lived with us, forty-eight came from a single-parent home. Only one teen had both natural parents. In spite of this fact, we still have parents who think divorce will not affect their children.

Divorce causes more problems than we are willing to recognize. Divorce is like a death, only we don't bury anyone. The Bible is clear: God hates divorce (Malachi 2:16). That does not mean God hates divorced people. He does not love you any less if you are divorced. God hates divorce because He knows the pain for you, your spouse, and the children will be real and intense; but all this can be avoided.

Good marriages don't just happen; they have to be worked at to be successful. All the couples whom I ministered to came with one agenda: "God, heal my marriage." It was always a challenge to convince those couples that God would not heal their marriages. He has never healed a marriage. The reason I can say that is because marriages don't get sick; people do. The question I always ask is, "Are you willing for God to change and heal you? Your marriage is fine; it's the two people in the marriage who need help and healing." I often say to people, "Don't try to heal your marriage; instead, try to get more intimate with God. The fruit of your closer relationship with Him is that your marriage will also be healed." Jesus said, "Seek first the Kingdom of God and His righteousness, and all these things will be added to you" (Matthew 6:33), which also includes marriage. The lesson is to put God first in every area of your life. For most of us, this is a process.

I am convinced, therefore, that most of those troubled teens would not have been in the state's care if their homes had been Christ-centered.

CHAPTER 9

COME APART AND LEARN OF ME

*I*t was also during our year with the teens that I began to hear a phrase resounding within my heart and my head. The phrase was, "I want you to come apart and learn of Me."

In 1980, I was working a full-time job managing a hog farm and doing outside sales for Clyde Betts & Sons, a farm supply store in Milton, Delaware. I had been employed there for about twenty-five years and never thought about doing anything else. I had a great wife and son and was actively involved in the Methodist church, hosting a Bible study every Thursday night. I was also ministering to an average of six status offender teens every week in our home. (The highest number of teens we had at any one time was nine.)

In the midst of all this, I was hearing, "I want you to come apart and learn of Me." I am sure the first time I heard this invitation, I paid no attention to it. Since this appeal from God kept recurring within my spirit over a period of twelve to eighteen months, however, I began to give thought as to what it meant. I gradually realized that God was saying to me, "I want you to go to a Bible school." This was somewhat scary, but not overwhelmingly so.

    I was sure there was some place I could attend that was close to home, or maybe I could even enroll in a correspondence school. My reluctance came from the nagging thought that maybe this was not God. I knew the Devil would not want me to go to Bible school, so perhaps my reluctance was just my flesh. The confirmation came, as it usually does, through prayer and other Christians.

JUST FILLING IN?

After eighteen months of struggling, I said, "Okay, Lord, if this is You, send someone to me to confirm that this is You; and if it is, I will go. I will do this." I prayed this prayer on a Wednesday, and the following Saturday the pastor's wife of the Methodist church I was attending called and said that her husband, Rev. Howard Evans, was sick and would not be able to attend the service on Sunday. She asked me as a lay leader to consider handling the service. I readily agreed and preached at the service.

Confirmation

On the Monday following the service, I received a phone call from Sonny Reed, a long-time friend and school classmate. He wanted to know if he could come over that night and talk to me. After he arrived and the small talk was over, he asked me, "When are you going to get on with what God is calling you to do?" I replied, "Why would you say that?"

He then talked about the great service we had on Sunday and that people were more important to God than pigs. I had never told anyone about what I thought I was hearing from God, so I took his words as a confirmation that I was to go to Bible school and learn of Him. Now, my question for God was, "Where to go?"

CHAPTER 11

WHERE TO GO?

*T*he first ones I told about my commitment to go to Bible school were Al and Laurene Bergez, friends of ours from the Lay Witness movement. As soon as I said I would go, Laurene said, "You should go to Rhema Bible Training Center in Tulsa, Oklahoma." My first response was, "No, there are Bible schools closer than Oklahoma. Let's pray about another one."

A few weeks later we went camping with the Bergez's at the now-defunct PTL Retreat Center in Charlotte, North Carolina. On the way down, we stopped to visit our long-time Christian friends, Paul and Sylvia Trollinger, in Asheboro, North Carolina. Paul, who was the president of the local Full Gospel Businessmen Association, invited us to stop on our way back home and be his guests at their Annual Ladies Night Banquet. They had special guests coming to speak and sing—the McFarland Family Singers from Oklahoma City, Oklahoma. We agreed and told Paul we'd see him in about a week.

While we were attending a financial management seminar at PTL, the speaker kept using the phrase, "This is a Rhema word." I did not know what a Rhema word was and was too proud to ask, so I sat there in ignorance. Finally, someone more humble than I spoke up and asked the question, "What is a Rhema word?" After the speaker finished giving a good explanation of what Rhema meant (which I will expound upon later), he added that it was also the name of a very good Bible school run by Kenneth Hagin in Tulsa, Oklahoma.

Prior to my conversation with the Bergez's about Rhema Bible Training Center, I had never heard of the place. Now, in a matter of weeks, I heard about it twice. On the way back to Delaware, we attended the Full Gospel Businessmen's Banquet in Asheboro and enjoyed the McFarland Family very much. After the meeting was over, we went to someone's home for some food and fellowship, and we got to enjoy one-on-one conversation with the McFarland's. Bob McFarland and I were in the kitchen getting acquainted and sharing about our lives, and I told him about my decision to attend a Bible school. He asked me where I was going, and I responded that I did not know. He immediately responded, "You should go to Rhema Bible Training Center in Tulsa. It's a great school."

Wow! That was the third confirmation!

Rhema It Is!

I decided that God was speaking to me in all of this, so I went home and found a Kenneth Hagin book with a mailing address in it and sent off a letter asking for information. When the material arrived, I filled out all the paperwork and walked to the mailbox to submit my application. As I put the envelope in the box, I prayed, "Lord, I believe this is You. If it is, I will go, but I really want to go this year. I can't wait another year."

This was already in August of 1980, and classes started the Tuesday after Labor Day. The dean of students called me at home about a week later and asked why my wife was not coming with me to school if I was accepted. They had never accepted a student whose spouse stayed home. I explained our reasons to him: We had an exceptionally strong marriage. Also, Mary Jane had worked twenty-five years as an administrative assistant with the State Department of Transportation, and she needed five more years to retire with a full pension. We thought it would be foolish for her to quit her job to go with me for just one year of Bible school.

They accepted me into the school but later told me that I was the only student they had ever accepted whose spouse did not go with him. I applaud their policy. I think the church sometimes is guilty of separating spouses, even for ministry purposes. That is the reason I always invite the spouse of a guest speaker at our church to be our guest as well.

After the second phone call which informed me I had been accepted but that classes would be starting in less than two weeks, the mad rush began. There were so many things I had to do to prepare for the time away from home. I purchased a little Ford Mustang from my brother and packed it to the brim for the journey. It was a sight to behold.

FOOT-WASHING

On the night before I left for Tulsa, while packing and attending to all the last-minute details, the phone rang. It was our friends Ronnie and Donna Mitchell. They wanted to come down and see us before I left. I said, "Yes," although I really did not think I had time for this. Boy, was I wrong!

They came in with all the equipment needed to wash feet, including perfume and oils. Ronnie said he was on a mission from God, and he was indeed. He shared how God had told him the previous Sunday to wash my and Mary Jane's feet to prepare us for the journey we were about to embark on. Even though Mary Jane would not be with me physically, Ronnie said that she would be with me every step of the way. He went on to say this was not just about Bible school, but it was a journey that we would walk together. Wow! What a night! We probably cried enough tears to wash our feet. There are many reasons the Mitchell's are so close to us, but this event wedded our hearts together in a special way. Thank you, Ronnie and Donna.

WESTWARD BOUND

The following morning, the Mustang and I began the long drive from Milton, Delaware, to Tulsa, Oklahoma. The first miles were a little blurry as I cried tears of sadness and loneliness, as well as tears of happiness and excitement.

After one crying spell, I looked in my rear-view mirror to see a Maryland state trooper motioning for me to pull over just before the Chesapeake Bay Bridge. I was doing 62 in a 55-mile-per-hour zone. As he was writing the ticket, he asked, "Where in the world are you going with all those clothes in the car?" Between sobs, I told him the story. When I finished, he tore up the ticket and said, "Watch your speed, and have a great year."

There would be many tears shed in the days ahead as I drove to class, crying tears of sadness because I missed Mary Jane and my family. But there were also tears of joy. For the first time in my life, I knew I was where God wanted me to be, doing what He wanted me to do in the place He had prepared for me.

If you have never experienced that kind of knowing, I pray that you will. There is no other feeling like it in the entire world.

CONFIRMATION . . . AGAIN

I received confirmation that I was indeed in the right place a few weeks later as I was leaving a Sunday morning service at Will Rogers United Methodist Church in Tulsa.

As I was exiting the church after the service, the pastor and his wife were standing by the door, greeting people as pastors often do. I greeted the pastor first, and then his wife, who was the closest to the exit door. As I let go of her hand, she re-gripped mine, which caused me to look back at her. She asked, "Do you have plans for Sunday dinner?"

Keep in mind that I had never been to that church before, had only been in Tulsa about two weeks, and I knew no one. I had visited the church hoping I would meet a Christian who had a room for rent. Because I had arrived later than most students at Rhema, all the student housing was taken. I was living in a motel, saying, "Lord, are you sure this is where You want me? I can't find a room."

An invitation for a meal was not the same as a room, but it was the best offer I had received all day. I immediately said yes, and she asked me to follow her to the parsonage, saying that the pastor would be along later. After arriving at the parsonage, she gave me the daily paper and went in the kitchen. After a few minutes, she stuck her head in the den and asked if I like Cornish hens. I replied that I did.

She said, "You're probably wondering what is going on and why I would invite you, a total stranger, for Sunday dinner." I told her the thought had crossed my mind. She replied that she didn't know either; but earlier that morning when she took two Cornish hens from the freezer, she heard God say, "Take out three. You are having company for dinner." She then asked the Lord, "Who?", and He replied, "I will show you." She continued, "When you shook my hand, I heard the Lord again, saying, "It's him. Invite him over for dinner."

After dinner I spent about three hours talking to her husband about the baptism of the Holy Spirit. The pastor's wife was baptized with the Holy Spirit, but he was not. He was a good man, a fine pastor and preacher; but he lacked the power of Pentecost that is readily available to us.

For months afterward, I was still thinking that this encounter was all about the pastor and his ministry and how God wanted to use me to speak into his life. WRONG! I sure hope that God did use me to speak into his life, but it was not about that at all. It was all about me. It was God's way of saying to me, "I know where you are, I know what you need, and I will provide it all in My time."

I think most of us who have forsaken much to follow after God need these encounters to give us bold assurance that we are indeed moving in the right direction. This was my personal 1 Kings 17 story.

1 KINGS 17

God will send ravens to meet your need, but we must be at the place God sends us. God's directions don't always make sense to the natural man. In the 1 Kings 17 story, after the brook dried up, God sent Elijah to a widow who had nothing to feed him—let alone herself or her son.

Why would God send a prophet like Elijah to someone who was down and out? Why not send him to a wealthy, prosperous person who had an abundance to meet his needs? The reason is that God's ways are higher than our ways. He wanted to bless both the widow woman and the man of God. Both had their needs met. Both were ministered to.

Incidentally, I found an apartment in Tulsa, about fifteen miles from Broken Arrow, the town where the Rhema campus is located. I shared a duplex with a bachelor named Bruce, who was a great guy and a wonderful landlord. Whenever Mary Jane visited me in Tulsa, he always gave her a warm welcome, perhaps because her cooking was a great asset to our bachelor living!

CHAPTER 17

THE SPOKEN WORD

Attending Rhema was a tremendous experience for me. Rhema is not a Bible college but a Bible training center where the students are taught the Word of God in an atmosphere of faith and love. The school was founded by the late Dr. Kenneth Hagin, whose life was changed and challenged by Mark 11:23-24. Thus, there was a strong emphasis on faith but also a well-balanced teaching centered on the lordship of Jesus.

Rhema has many critics. I found that I disagreed with some of the students about what they thought they heard taught, but I did not disagree with what I was hearing. Rhema has erroneously been called a "name it and claim it school" or a "blab it and grab it school" because of the emphasis put on the value of the spoken word. They taught the Word, however, without apology. I learned that the Bible is full of illustrations that instruct us about what we say.

Jesus said that the Word of God is like seed (Mark 4 and Luke 8), and our human hearts are like the soil. The seed determines what kind of fruit will come forth, and the soil is the deciding factor regarding how much is produced. When God created the earth, He used words, speaking it into existence. Hebrews 11:3 says, "And God said, 'Let it be' and it was" (emphasis added). Words determine our direction in life (James 3:1-10). It is one thing hearing truth taught in class, but it is quite another learning experience when it is fleshed out in our lives.

BEING WHERE GOD WANTS YOU

The reality of how powerful the Word is became real to me—not in school, but in the crucible of life. God gave me clear directions in my journey about traveling with Earl Tyson, including His command to me not to accept any money from Earl's ministry. I began to travel with Earl in August of 1981. In December of that same year, I began to get nervous. My checkbook began to agree with my critics' assessment of my life, which was in the natural. You can't make it. My common sense also agreed. We had almost $2,000 in bills coming due by the year's end, and a $100 check would have overdrawn our account. I began to panic and fuss with God. I said things such as, "God, I have never been late in my life on a payment. What am I going to do?" During my time of anguish, God directed me to read the story of Peter getting out of the boat (Matthew 14:22-32). It was as though I had never read the story before.

I saw many things that I had never seen. For one, the disciples were in the boat, crossing over the Sea of Galilee, not because they thought it was a good idea or even a nice day for a boat ride. They were in the boat because of Jesus' direction. They were exactly where God (Jesus) told them to be. This is very important.

The next thing I realized for the first time was what Jesus was doing while they were being tossed about in the sea. He was on the mountain, praying for them (v. 23).

After visiting this place myself, I believe that He probably could see them from the mountainside and sense their anxiety. The word "fear" is not used until they saw Him walking on the water and thought that He was a ghost. Then, they cried out in fear. Jesus identified Himself and said, "Don't be afraid." Peter replied, "If it is You, bid me to come to You." And Jesus replied, "Come." Then Peter got down out of the boat, walked on the water, and came toward Jesus. But when he saw the wind, he was afraid, and beginning to sink, cried out, "Lord, save me!" Immediately, Jesus reached out His hand and caught him. "You of little faith," he said, "why did you doubt?"

I always had known that Jesus comes to us in our storms of life. But I saw for the first time that Peter did not walk on the water; instead, he walked on the Word. Jesus said, "Come." The water did not support Peter; the Word from Jesus did. I also saw that it was only when Peter took his eyes off of Jesus and refocused them on the winds and waves that he began to sink. He then cried out to Jesus, "Lord, save me!" Then Jesus extended His hand to Peter, picked him back up, and placed him on top of his circumstances—the water and wind. I believe they both walked back to the boat, hand in hand. The Bible says that when they got into the boat, the wind ceased.

I then applied this story to my situation. As I reviewed the facts, I knew that I was in the boat that Jesus had instructed me to get in. In other words, I was where God had told me to go, doing what He had told me to do. I did not have just a word; I had a whole discourse telling me what to do and with whom to do it.

I also realized that my concern came from my narrow focus on finances and other circumstances—in other words, on the winds and waves. I had taken my eyes off of Jesus. I also now knew that if I cried out, "Jesus save me," He would. So, I did and He did. I went and got all of my bills, put them in the middle of the floor, and said, "Lord, I don't know much, but I know that I am where You told me to be, doing what You told me to do; therefore, these are Your bills, not mine." I stood on them and received His peace.

Every dime that we needed came to us before the end of the year from unimaginable sources—Christian and non-Christian. All of our needs were met. During this time, I experienced a healing in the area of finances. I never again fretted about money. Now, my only concern is this: Am I where God wants me to be, doing what He wants me to do? If so, the rest is up to Him.

Two Words

The Bible speaks of two different kinds of words from God: the logos word and the rhema word. Both are extremely important. The logos word is the written Word of God, and the rhema word is the spoken word of God. The rhema word may come to us through the logos, a vision, dream, or a prophetic utterance.

Have you ever been reading the Bible, and a word seems to leap off of the page at you? This is the logos becoming the rhema. This is what I call "the Word" becoming "a word" to me. We must let the Holy Spirit make the Word alive to us. He wants to! Using the Manufacturer's handbook can enable us to miss a lot of grief and frustration in our walk through life.

Read the Book!

CHAPTER 19

THE SCHOOL YEAR

After moving into my Delaware Avenue apartment and finding a part-time job cutting grass at a local country club, I began to settle into school. People have often asked me about school, my favorite class, or the one thing I learned that was most important to me.

There were many great experiences, classes, and instructors. Yet, the most important thing was not any one class but the fact that for one year I did nothing else but learn of Jesus. Through His Word, I got to know Him! It's not that I know everything about Him; I don't. But for one year, I was able to separate myself from the world and concentrate on learning more about Jesus while also getting to really know Him. I am still learning and building on that year of study to get to know Him. Don't skim over this truth. I think a lot of poor theology stems from a poor awareness of God, His character, and attributes.

If we know someone, we know what they will or will not do. After being married to Mary Jane over fifty years, if someone told me they saw her coming out of a bar, I would know they are mistaken because I know my wife. God wants us to know Him like that.

God cannot give you what He does not have. When people ask questions like "Why did God put cancer on them?" it makes me wonder if they know God at all. If you know Jesus, you know He came to heal people, not to make them sick. It is His nature. It is Who He is.

One of the major reasons we don't know God as we should is that the Revealer of God is the Holy Spirit, and Jesus is the express image of God Himself (Hebrews 1:3). If we reject the full ministry of the Holy Spirit, we have rejected the only way to know Him. Jesus Himself said that the Holy Spirit would talk about Him as He shares what the Father reveals to Him. It's not that Christians don't believe in the Holy Spirit; instead, we often just want to pick and choose what the work of the Holy Spirit is. The most important function of the Holy Spirit does not involve the gifts He gives or the fruit He enables us to produce. It is His primary role to reveal Jesus. So, be hungry for the fullness of the Holy Spirit so that Jesus will become more real to you than your best friend (John 15:13-15).

I personally think some of the most damaging teaching in the body of Christ is that upon your salvation, you have all of the Holy Spirit that there is to receive. Jesus did not think so.

I believe that our pattern for Christian living and ministry should be Jesus. When Jesus presented Himself to John for water baptism, I am thoroughly convinced that He had the Holy Spirit.

He was conceived by the Holy Spirit, so He was Emmanuel—God with us, God in human flesh. He lived on this earth after taking on the likeness of sinful flesh.

In the account of Jesus' water baptism in Luke 3, we read that the Holy Spirit descended upon Him in bodily form (v. 21-22). If we receive all the Holy Spirit there is to get in salvation, what was this event all about? I believe it was about empowering for ministry. Jesus was about thirty years of age at this event, yet He had not begun His public ministry. Why? Was He waiting until He was thirty, or was He waiting for the empowering that only the Holy Spirit could give?

Notice that immediately after this event, He spent forty days in the wilderness and then began His ministry. I believe the Scriptures teach that this is the same pattern He prescribed for the disciples. In John 20, after His resurrection, He appeared to them in the Upper Room and said, "Peace." Then He breathed on them and said, "Receive ye the Holy Spirit." I truly believe that they all received the Holy Spirit at that time. But they were also the same disciples whom He spoke to in Acts 1: "Don't begin your ministry until you go down to Jerusalem and wait for the promise of the Father I told you about and John told you about. Not many days from now you will be baptized with the Holy Spirit" (paraphrased).

Notice that this was not a suggestion or recommendation. He commanded them. Also notice that between His resurrection and the Day of Pentecost the disciples did not minister. As a matter of fact, it looks like they were going back to their old vocations. Peter said, "I'm going fishing" (John 21:3, NLT). Thomas, Nathaniel, James, John, and two of the other disciples with them said, "So are we."

I don't think they were just fishing for that night's dinner. I think they were discouraged and wanted their old, familiar lives back, yet they obeyed Him. After Pentecost, it was an entirely different story because they were an entirely different bunch of disciples. The hundred and twenty in that upper room changed the entire world. That event is still greatly affecting lives today. It surely has had a significant impact on mine.

Thank God for Pentecost! Pentecost is not just a day on a church calendar; it is a vital experience that every believer needs. It can happen five minutes after salvation, or twenty years later, but it needs to happen for the church to possess the power it needs to be His witnesses in Jerusalem (that's your home), in Judea (that's your county), and Samaria (those you don't like as much), and then to the ends of the earth (Acts 1:8). So, to know Him is crucial to our walk with God and our ministry with Him.

I took many classes at Rhema that ministered to me deeply. There were none that were dull or boring. Every instructor at the school was especially anointed of God to teach their particular classes. Many of them would pray for one or two hours before each class. What a commitment!

I hesitate to single out any particular class since they were all so good, but two classes were extremely important to me because I understood so little about these subjects. I want to share an experience about one class called "Righteousness" because during the ten years I traveled with an evangelist, I discovered that many other people in the church didn't understand this subject either.

I received so much from this ninety-minute class on righteousness held three times a week that when it ended, I thought I understood righteousness. Several weeks after this class was over, however, I was working on a lawnmower in the shop at Indian Springs Country Club, minding my own business. Suddenly I realized that I WAS THE RIGHTEOUSNESS OF GOD IN CHRIST JESUS!

This was not a "head thing" but an illumination of the revelation that the Holy Spirit gives. Psalm 119:130 says, "The entrance of God's Word brings light." You see, we don't understand God's Word; we see God's Word through the Holy Spirit. I began to shout and share what I had just come to understand to some other Rhema students working at the country club, but nobody else seemed to be excited about what I had just realized. The reason was that they had not seen what I had seen. The logos word recorded in 2 Corinthians 5:21 had just become a rhema word for me, and I would be forever changed. I share this because I believe that all of the Word must become a word to us. The Bible stops becoming logos—pen and ink or just a book—when the Holy Spirit illuminates it within our spirit. It will change us. Indeed, it will change our world.

The other class that was so powerful to me was called "The Blood Covenant." I always did have many questions about the blood; in fact, I had many more questions than answers. I want everyone to know that I still have questions. The more answers I get, the more questions come. That is why this Christian life is such an exciting journey, and it is a journey. This class taught me much, but it also made me hungry for more. So, I am still seeking to know more about the blood.

The pivotal verse about the blood is Leviticus 17:11 (Amplified): "For the life (the animal soul) is in the blood, and I have given it for you upon the altar to make atonement for your souls; for it is the blood that makes atonement by reason of the life [which it represents]." Now, whenever I read the word "blood" in the Scriptures, I substitute the word "life." I would encourage you to do the same.

Life during the school year was simply great! I drove about fifteen miles to school each morning, crying most of the time because I missed my wife and family, but all the while experiencing joy on the inside. This was a new experience for me; however, I knew for the first time in my life that I was in the will of God. Any doubts I harbored had left after my visit to Will Rogers United Methodist Church and the dinner afterward with the pastor and his wife.

Shortly after classes began, I sat in the chapel service one day and met fellow student, Terry Whetstone, who was working at the Indian Springs Country Club on the grounds-keeping crew. He said they were looking for more help. (Rhema classes were scheduled so that you could work part-time if needed.) I applied and was hired on the crew. It was a godsend for me. There were several Rhema students working there, and we began to influence the place in a positive way. We even had the privilege of praying the sinner's prayer with the superintendent, Chuck Hybl. His house soon became a hangout for all the crew and became a home away from home for all of us.

About mid-way through the year, while sitting in a class taught by Dr. Ken Stewart, my instructor made a statement that really troubled me and hindered me from hearing anything else. I really don't remember what his point was, but he said that God did not have a permissive will—only one perfect will. This was an area I had not visited before this. When he made that statement, I was also taking a class on suffering; and we were, among other things, studying the Book of Job.

I was sure Dr. Stewart was wrong. Because the whole student body—about two thousand students—attended his class, however, you could not get to him to discuss the subject any further. I asked the instructor of the Job class about it. He wisely replied that he did not know the context Dr. Stewart was speaking in, but suggested that I ask the Holy Spirit to reveal the answer to me. That was good advice. I wonder now why I didn't think of that. So I began a journey seeking an answer to the question, "Does God have both a perfect will and a permissive will?"

Several days later, I was driving to work at the country club, praying in the Spirit and asking God, "Do you have a permissive will?" Suddenly, God was speaking to me—not audibly, but just as real. I heard God say to my spirit, "I am a perfect God, and I have one perfect will. What the world calls My permissive will is really their ability to choose. There is a great difference between Me allowing something and them causing it because of their choices."

WOW! I had my answer, straight from the Holy Spirit. I think it was the following day when I decided to stop for a burger on the way to work. As I went in to eat and was looking for a table (bless God!), in one of the booths sat Dr. Ken Stewart, all alone. I went over with my tray, introduced myself, and asked if I could join him. During lunch I shared with him what his statement had done to me and asked if he could explain to me what he meant. I did not tell him that I had already heard from God. It was amazing that the answer he gave me was almost word for word what the Holy Spirit had shared with me. Years later, in August of 1999, when we dedicated our new thousand-seat sanctuary at Eagle's Nest Fellowship, we were honored that Dr. Stewart participated in the services.

Before my classes started in the fall of 1981, I was really nervous about going back to school at my age and learning to study all over again and applying the same kind of commitment to get good grades. After all, I had graduated from high school in 1954, and it had been a long time since I had been a student. I learned something valuable during this time. All the classes were lectures; and since I could not ask questions or tape the classes, I took good notes. Because my handwriting needs help, I would transcribe the notes each night after class, work, and dinner before they got cold. Then I would turn on the cassette recorder to highlight notes from each class and send the tape to Mary Jane. I discovered that writing the notes twice and speaking them once made all of my tests a breeze. I got good grades without having to cram for exams.

Tulsa was (and still is) like a Christian smorgasbord. There was someone in town all the time. All the top Christian leaders and teachers in the nation came to the churches or the convention center, and it was difficult not to try to attend them all. So, I constantly had to remind myself of the reason I was there.

The years of 1980 and 1981 were exciting times in the body of Christ. Oral Roberts was building the City of Faith, and many of our students worked part-time over there. We all were invited to many special events at the Oral Roberts University Mabee Center. I also attended the very first service of Victory Christian Center, led by founding pastor Billy Joe Daugherty in a vacant car dealership on Easter Sunday, 1981. Mary Jane was able to go with me because God provided finances for her to fly out and spend Easter with me.

THE CALL TO MINISTRY

An event that changed my life forever happened in January of 1981. I have never had trouble sleeping, so it was strange and new to me to begin waking up at 2:30 or 3:00 every morning. For the first few times it happened, I thought I should pray for Mary Jane and my family back home; so I did, but that did not seem to give me any release. For two to three weeks, I continued to awaken at about the same hour. Frankly, it was getting old.

On January 21st, I awoke in the middle of the night as usual and found myself fussing with God again. I said in frustration, "Lord, I am going to school full time, working forty hours a week at the country club, and now You are waking me up at 2:30 every morning. I can't stand it. I need my rest. What is going on? Are You trying to tell me something?" I guess the Lord had been waiting for me all along to ask Him why He was waking me. Because of my slowness to inquire, I lost a few weeks of sleep.

The Lord answered in a voice I had learned to recognize, simply saying, "Yes, it concerns your ministry." I replied, "What ministry?" He said, "I want you to travel with Earl Tyson for two years. You are not to take any money from his ministry. I will meet your needs in other ways. I want you to learn how to minister to people one on one."

I asked, "Lord, what will I be doing with him? I don't preach, I don't teach, and I certainly don't sing." The Lord replied, "Carry his bags if that is all he asks you to do, but go and learn how to minister one on one."

I said, "Lord, does Earl know this?" He replied, "No, but he will when you tell him." I said, "Lord, to confirm this discussion, heal my tennis elbow." Instantly, the constant pain in my elbow left. (I had torn a muscle in my left arm loading feeder pigs onto a trailer before I left the farm, and the doctors called it tennis elbow. I had received two shots for the pain and was told that one more was all they could give me, and then surgery would be necessary.) God had other plans. He truly is "the Lord who healeth thee" (Acts 4:10).

WOW! I don't know how else to describe this experience. I had none like it ever before and none to date, and it was life-changing for my family and me. I did not know when I left home what God had in store for me after Bible school, but I assumed that I would just "learn of Him" and go back to the pig farm. Apparently, God had other plans.

CHAPTER 21

REFLECTIONS FROM THE FARM

As I reflect back on my life, I know now that most of the time I just went wherever there was the least resistance. I never had any goals or long-range plans, nor did I ever think that God had a plan, a purpose, and a place that He wanted me to be. As I look back on the events of my life before attending Bible school, ending up at Clyde Betts & Son was really a godsend for me. I started my job working with outside sales for this family-owned farm supply center. They were Purina dealers, Oliver Farm Equipment dealers, and Dekalb seed and fertilizer dealers. They also offered on-the-farm hammer mill grinding service.

After working there for a few years, my employers became like an extended family to Mary Jane and me. Owner and founder Clyde Betts, an excellent businessman with high moral character, became my first mentor. He always treated people fairly, and he and his wife, Catherine, treated me as family. My relationships with his son Harold, his wife Jackie, his daughter Donna, and her husband Ronnie, were very special. We became very close and precious friends as we all grew spiritually together with our children. Harold and Jackie's son, Rick, was our first worship leader at Eagle's Nest Fellowship Church, and he is currently the pastor of Crossroads Community Church near Bridgeville, Delaware.

I was the one who encouraged Clyde Betts & Son to get started in the swine business. They already were in the chicken business and had about twenty thousand laying hens producing table eggs, but Clyde realized we needed to diversify. He kept asking me to attend meetings that Purina held about the swine business, and we eventually bought sixteen feeder pigs to fatten up for slaughter. This marked the beginning of Clyde Betts & Son entering the swine business in the early seventies. By the time I left the farm for Bible school, we had grown into a five hundred sow farrow-to-finish operation that produced almost two hundred new piglets each week.

I enjoyed the challenge of developing the hog farm. In the process, I also learned some valuable lessons in life and made new friends. I guess I have always been an entrepreneur, and I tried many new methods in the swine business. We were among the first to have a confinement hog center, and we even started weaning pigs at twenty-one days of age—something no one else was doing except in research centers. I developed a friendship with Dr. Richard Fowler, the swine specialist at the University of Delaware, and he worked closely with me as we tried out several innovative techniques.

I discovered that there are many similarities between people and pigs. One of the first things I learned is that both pigs and people get from Point A to Point B much easier if we lead them rather than drive them. If you rattle a feed bucket and walk in front of them, pigs will follow you anywhere—even to market. People are like that. As a pastor, I've learned to feed them with the Bible, and they follow me.

I also learned that when pigs get out of the lots in which they have been cooped up by crawling under the fence, they do not want to go back in through the gate, even if you open it wide for them. It is much easier to get them to go back through the hole that they got out of. This is a good lesson for people also. When people get out of fellowship with God, they need to go back to the place where they got out by repenting and getting back into fellowship with God.

We also employed animal science students from the University of Delaware on the farm. I remember one student who challenged me about a statement I made as I was sharing about Jesus with her. She replied, "I don't believe that." I replied, "OK. I do, and I believe it because the Bible says so. On what do you base your unbelief?" I received no answer. I had the privilege to lead her to the Lord before the summer's end. Praise God!

That same life on the farm is what I thought I was coming back to, but the Lord had other plans. I knew I had to call Earl.

I never told anyone except Mary Jane about my message from God. I did not want to talk to Earl about it over the phone, so I decided to wait until I went home over spring break. Between

January and March, I experienced many spiritual battles with the Devil. I think most of us question what we hear when we believe we have heard from God. I went home in March on spring break, anxiously waiting to tell Earl what I had heard; but I wasn't sure what his response would be.

After arriving home and calling Earl, I discovered that he was not home. He was traveling around the country ministering and would not be back until the day before I had to go back to school. Earl lives about three hundred miles from me, so I was forced to have the conversation by phone. I'm not sure what I was expecting, but it was not what I got!

When I told Earl the Lord had instructed me to travel with him, he laughed (yes, laughed) and asked me when I had received that word. I told him it was January 21st. He replied that back in November or December he had been flying to a Camp Farthest Out meeting in Seattle, Washington. He was about to take a nap when he said a thought came to him in the form of a statement: "I want you to begin to travel and minister with a layman." He said he had first dismissed the statement by protesting, "Lord, I've been alone all these years. I don't need to travel with someone."

Earl said that after he heard the statement a second time, he responded, "OK, Lord, if this is You, I will do it; but I am not going to look for someone. You send them to me." Earl then told me that on the basis of what I just shared with him, he would trust God that I was the one He was sending to him.

I thought God had said that Earl would know when I told him. What He really meant was that Earl would know that I was the one when I told him. Earl then asked when I would graduate, and I told him in June 1981. I would then be able to go with him beginning that late summer or fall. After we began traveling together, Earl shared from the pulpit about how God had put us together. He would often say, "You know it had to be God, because if I had picked someone it would have been a lawyer from Des Moines, Iowa, not a pig farmer from Delaware."

FLESHING OUT THE CALL

I went with Earl to my first revival meeting in August of 1981. I have to admit that this was even more frightening than going to Bible school. I really did not know Earl that well, and I was concerned about what this would really be like. What would I do, and how would the people accept me? My fears were put to rest early as people seemed to accept me, mainly because Earl endorsed and accepted me.

The Holy Spirit's Role

Earl had a way of telling stories, usually personal ones, which made the Scriptures come alive. His love for Jesus and people was contagious; therefore, he was well accepted, as was I, wherever we went.

It was under Earl's ministry that Mary Jane and I received the baptism of the Holy Spirit in the Methodist church, which I have already shared about. Because he ministered in the anointing and power of the Holy Spirit and talked about the Person and work of the Holy Spirit so much, there were several instances when people would disagree with him. Yet, I think because he was real and lived what he preached, even those people whose theology was different were drawn to him.

I believe that people will accept you and give you their ear if they are convinced you are real and have paid a price for what you believe. For instance, I don't agree with Nelson Mandela on many issues, but I will listen to him because he has paid a price for his beliefs and convictions.

I believe that is one reason Earl was regularly invited to speak and minister in so many places. I also believe that is why they accepted me. I think there was a small minority who thought I was a wealthy, retired hog farmer from Delaware who had nothing better to do than roam around the country with this Southern evangelist, but most knew the truth because Earl would tell them.

I also believe that even though Earl's official title within the United Methodist Church was a "conference evangelist," calling Earl an evangelist was a misnomer. Earl was called by God to go to the local churches that were dead and stagnant and had not seen God move in their midst in the last fifty, or sometimes, one hundred years. A lot of these people were saved, though many were not. Somehow in their journey, they became satisfied and petrified.

It reminds me of the story I have told many times about the little boy who kept falling out of bed each night. After nothing she did seemed to work, the mother asked, "Son, why do you keep falling out of bed?" He replied, "I don't know, Mother. It must be because I fall asleep too close to where I got in." I think this is what has happened to many members of our churches: They got in (saved) and then fell asleep (they were satisfied and petrified).

Earl's call was to shake them so they would wake up. This he did quite effectively. We were mostly invited to Methodist churches because Earl was an ordained evangelist in the Virginia Conference of the United Methodist Church, but we were asked to visit other congregations as well.

I think the saddest situations we observed were Pentecostal churches that were also satisfied. This experience taught me that no matter where you are in your walk with God, you have not exhausted all that God has for you.

I also noticed during my travels with Earl that people were frightened and often opposed to whatever they had not experienced in the Kingdom. We were preaching and teaching at one Midwest church in a college town and had a tremendous revival. It was a fairly large church with multiple pastors on staff. During the week we saw many people come to the Lord, others baptized with the Holy Spirit, and many marriages healed. The whole family I stayed with was converted during the week. The pastor told us later that the church board was discussing having us both back the next year, but there was opposition to this after the Christian education director asked the question, "What are you going to do with all these people who get born again if you invite them back?"

When I heard that report, I realized that people oppose what they have not encountered. People need an encounter with God instead of just head knowledge or mental assent to the Word of God.

John Wesley, the founder of Methodism, said that there was a thief in church called mental assent. We may intellectually say, "I believe," but nothing ever changes in our lives. The word "belief" comes from two words: "by" and "life." If you really believe, I will be able to tell it by your life. The world is longing to see the church walk the talk. For so long now, too many inconsistencies exist in the lives of people in our pews week after week. On Sundays, they're praying, clapping, shouting, and even jumping, then they live like the rest of the community the other days of the week. We need to realize that we will only transform the world after we have allowed the Holy Spirit to transform us.

EARL'S SONG

I had many personal experiences that shaped my life during the ten years I spent with Earl. Early on I realized that Earl was really like a song looking for a place to be sung. What do I mean by that? I mean that he woke up each morning with a song in his heart and coming out of his mouth, and he went to bed the same way: singing. I think he knew every verse of every song in the Methodist hymnal, as well as most of the choruses that the Charismatic movement was singing. He is a lover of people. Amazingly, in ten years of ministry with him, I never heard the same sermon twice. He would use the same Scripture passage, but he always told different stories to illustrate it.

Identity Crisis

One of the first churches I visited with Earl was in Roanoke, Virginia. It happened to be the last church Earl had pastored before becoming an evangelist, so he knew a lot of the people there. We had been invited to stay with two older ladies who were longtime friends of Earl and his wife Betty. They had decided to have a dinner party on Saturday night before the Sunday through Thursday revival services began the next morning. Earl was scheduled to preach and I was slated to teach a Bible study for the adult classes during Sunday school.

I soon realized that Roanoke was considered a center for the educated elite in Virginia. At this dinner party there were several Ph.D.'s, two Rhodes Scholars, and I think all of the rest had a minimum of a Master's degree. So, here I was with a Ph.D. in scoop shovels, and I was going to teach them the Bible the next morning! I have never felt so inadequate in all my life.

They all treated me fine, but the Devil was sure beating me up about my lack of education. About halfway through the evening, I made a decision. I would return home the next morning. I knew I had nothing to teach them because they all were smarter than I was, so I planned to spend the night, arise early the next morning, and head back to Delaware.

After dinner and some great fellowship, our hostess announced that she had baked a special loaf of bread for the evening. It was to be used for Communion before we began the week of services at the church. She had already asked Earl to preach the Communion service. Seated in a circle in their dining room, we listened to Earl share a brief message. After he consecrated the elements, he broke the loaf and passed the two halves around the circle for each of us to break off a piece. He then did likewise with the chalice. This was not intinction (dipping the bread in the cup); we all drank from the one common cup. As the cup was passed to me, I heard the Lord say within my spirit, "This is what qualifies you to speak for Me. I have not called you to be an expert; I have called you to be My witness." In that instant, I knew that I was to stay and not go home.

Two of the most precious people I had the joy of getting to know that week were guests at the dinner party: Baxter and Anna Mow. They had retired after many years of missionary work in China. Baxter became a teacher of Hebrew to seminary students. (He could speak Hebrew better than I could speak English!) Anna was a gifted speaker and authored many books on the Holy Spirit. Both of them were Ph.D.'s, who, just by that fact alone, intimidated me very much early on. I fell in love with them, however, and spent time in their home all week. What a joy! I recall this event, which was the initial healing of my identity, whenever I don't feel adequate for the job at hand (like writing a book).

A few years after this event, Earl and I were on a mission trip with Rick Bonfim, a Brazilian evangelist from the North Georgia Conference. We all preached, taught, and ministered at various venues in Rio de Janeiro, São Paulo, and several other cities in Brazil.

Earl and I went one evening to a condominium in Copacabana Beach which a wealthy businesswoman owned and maintained just for Full Gospel Bible studies. No one actually lived there. It was located on the tenth floor of a high-rise and reeked of money. Rick had asked me to teach, and I felt led to speak on the person and work of the Holy Spirit. About fifty people were there, and the hostess served as the interpreter, speaking English fluently.

At the conclusion of my teaching, I gave an invitation to those who wanted to receive the baptism of the Holy Spirit. Five men who were seated on the first row slid out of their chairs and knelt in front of me, and I prayed for them. Each one of them received the Spirit, with the evidence of tongues. I later learned that they were all nuclear physicists, visiting Rio to attend a conference. I could not help but think about what a sense of humor God has—to use a small-town Delaware pig farmer to lay hands on five Ph.D.'s in Brazil and minister to them. This occurred because of the healing I received in Roanoke, Virginia.

There really is an identity crisis in the body of Christ. We need to receive and live in the awareness of both whose and who we are in Him. We are who Jesus says we are, whether we live like it or not and whether we feel like it or not. What God the Father said to Jesus the Son at His water baptism when the Holy Spirit came upon Him and remained He longs to say to each of us: "You are My beloved son (or daughter) and in you I am well pleased."

I am convinced that the temptation the Devil first challenged Jesus with is one he continues to use on us. It was not to turn stone to bread; it was to doubt what God had declared. Notice that the Devil began with the question, "If You are the Son of God, turn these stones to bread. You are hungry, aren't You?" Look at Jesus' response. In so many words, He said, "Man does not live by bread alone, but he lives by every word that comes from the mouth of God. And the words that come from the mouth of God say that I am His beloved Son; therefore, I know who I am because

I heard God say so—not because I turn stones to bread."

We need to make a lifestyle of confessing the same things that Jesus confesses about us. For example, we can declare, "I am saved. I am healed. I am the righteousness of God in Christ Jesus. I am more than a conqueror in Him." What we say controls the direction for our lives.

I thought I had found my niche managing the hog operation for Clyde Betts & Son, Inc. in Milton. Here I am fueling the truck for one of my regular runs to the market in Lancaster, PA. The building behind me later become the first home of Eagle's Nest Fellowship Church, and is presently the Eagle's Nest Day Care.

This photo was taken at Eagle's Nest Campground during our first fundraising auction in the early 1980's.

Mary Jane and I were privileged to host several trips to the Holy Land, along with Earl and Betty Tyson. It was amazing to walk where Jesus walked, while enjoying the teaching & insight of Earl along the way.

Graduation Day finally arrived, and I completed my year of study at Rhema Bible Training Center. The adventure was just beginning.

My son, Bill Jr., started Delaware's first Christian radio station, and I co-hosted a weekly call-in talk show with Pastor Dale Mast for several years.

One of my favorite things to do as a pastor is dedicate babies. This one was extra special because I was dedicating my first great grandson, Riley Sammons.

One of my favorite Bible teachers is Pastor Jack Hayford, founding pastor of the Church on the Way in Van Nuys, CA. I attended a conference at his church, and learned he is an authentic and genuine individual.

I suppose most men would say their first car was their favorite. It definitely was in my case. Here I am, sitting proudly in my 1940 Ford Coupe.

At the end of 2007, I officially retired as Senior Pastor of Eagle's Nest, and passed the mantle to Pastor Bob Weed who is now leading the church and continuing our mission of reaching Sussex County for Christ.

Mary Jane was able to come visit me in Tulsa during my year studying at Rhema. Those days always came and went much too fast.

I never dreamed that 25 years after graduating from Milton High School, I would once again be wearing a robe and graduating from a bible training center and starting a new career & ministry.

I wish I had room to share pictures with the hundreds of people who have supported, encouraged and prayed for me over the years. These 3 precious ladies are Jane Phillips, Stella Jester and Marge Camenisch. Marge is the one who gave me the title for this book.

I grew up and graduated from high school with Sonny Reed. Later we both became Christians, and God allowed our paths to merge many years later at Eagle's Nest Fellowship Church. It is my honor to dedicate this book to Sonny.

On August 24, 2006, Mary Jane and I celebrated our 50th Wedding Anniversary with several hundred friends and family. Participating in the ceremony were John Hobbs and Carl Vincent, two of our dear friends.

CHAPTER 24

KEEP PRAYIN'!

During the ten years I traveled with Earl, even though there were many disappointments, there were also many things that encouraged me. One was the fact that every church we visited always had a remnant of hungry people who longed for more of God and were open to a fresh move of God in their midst. If I had to pick the most outstanding week, it would be the week we spent at a church in Decatur, Illinois.

Earl had been invited because the senior pastor had heard him speak at a Camp Farthest Out meeting. His congregation once was a United Brethren Church before the United Brethren and Methodist churches merged to become the United Methodist Church. This was a fairly large church with four pastors on the staff. The senior pastor had agreed at Earl's request to allow me to teach the Bible studies and Rick Bonfim to lead the praise and worship for the week of services, even though he did not know us or anything about us.

We arrived in Decatur on Saturday, and the pastor asked the three of us to join his staff for dinner at a local steak house. After dinner, he suggested that we go by the church and pray for the services during the week. Rick led us in some praise and worship; then we began to pray and anoint the pews, choir loft, and pulpit with oil, inviting the Holy Spirit to have His way for the week. After we had blessed the entire sanctuary, the pastor asked us if Earl, Rick, and I would pray for and anoint the staff of the church and their spouses who were with them. They knelt at the altar, and we began to pray for each pastor and their spouses. Even before I began to pray, I heard Rick at my left say, "In the name of Jesus, I command this lustful, whoring spirit to come out and to come out now!"

I remember thinking, "This is not a good way to start a week of services" as I looked up at Rick, who had laid his hands on the head of the senior pastor's wife! Rick then realized what he had just said, looked her in the eye, and said, "Sister, I may be out of order." She replied, "You're not; keep prayin'."

Wow! What honesty! What openness and transparency! We went on to have a week of tremendous ministry at that church, and I am confident it all hinged on her response to Rick: "You're not; keep prayin'." As a result of this time, we decided to meet in the pastor's office each morning before Bible study to pray. On Monday morning as we were praying and sharing, I heard the Lord say within my spirit, "I want you to wash the senior pastor's feet." I dismissed the thought, not knowing whether he would be offended or not, or even agree to a foot-washing. When the thought came the second time, I decided that I would rather offend the pastor than the Holy Spirit, so I spoke what I had heard. His response was, "If that is what you heard, we'd better do it."

The worship leader said he had a basin in his office that he had used to water some plants that morning. He was back with us shortly, and I proceeded to wash the pastor's feet, not knowing why. At the beginning of the Wednesday night service, the reason became clear. The pastor began by asking me to forgive him. He shared with the congregation how he had told Earl at first that it was all right for Rick and I to come, but when he saw in my biography where I had gone to Bible school, he cried out, "Oh no!" He confessed, "I have written books against that school." He then said as he pointed at me, "I want this congregation to know that he has opened the Bible to me in a way no other human being has, and it is a joy to be taught by him." This was another miracle. We also saw many salvations and healings that week.

On Thursday, our final day there, we were in the pastor's office for the morning prayer time, and the pastor said he was not going to let me leave until he washed my feet. As he was finishing the foot-washing and prayers, there was a knock on the door. Earl, being the closest, opened the door. There stood a dirty, disheveled man. Earl asked, "What can I do for you, brother?" He said, "I'm dead. I am a dead man." Earl replied, "Come on in here. You are not dead. You are just getting ready to live."

He sat in the chair that I had been sitting in to get my feet washed and began to tell us his story. He had been a successful businessman but through poor choices ended up on the streets after he had lost everything, including his family. He said he had been walking down the street across from the church when he had an urge to go in and see the pastor. As he crossed the street to enter the church, he heard a voice that said, "If you go in there, I will kill you." He said the urge to go was stronger, so he came on in the church. He stopped at the receptionist's desk, where he was told the pastor was busy and could not be disturbed. He said that while the receptionist turned her back, he found the pastor's office and knocked on the door. He repeated, "I guess I am a dead man."

Earl replied again, "No, you are just getting ready to live for the first time in your life." Earl slid the basin over, took off the man's shoes and socks, and began to wash his feet. The pastor joined him, washing one foot while Earl washed the other. When they had finished, I opened my Bible and began to read Scriptures to him concerning salvation.

Using what we call "The Roman Road" (Romans 3:23; 6:23; 5:18; and 10:13), I led this man to the Lord; and he prayed with me eagerly. He knew this was a divine encounter. After we finished praying, Rick Bonfim came over, laid hands on his head, and proceeded to pray and take authority over the darkness that this man had given himself over to. After five or six demons had left this man, he was a sight to behold. There he sat in dirty, ragged clothes with his pants rolled up to his knees, barefooted, and his hair matted down on his forehead because of all the oil we had poured on his head. But he had light in his eyes for the first time.

He gazed at us and then looked around the room. He said, "What is today?" Earl gave him the day, month, and year. He said, "This is the first day of my life." Amen!

We left him in the hands of the pastor and the church. I have since thought about the process of what happened to him. How did it start? I believe it started when the senior pastor's wife said, "Keep prayin'." I believe it was the power of God in the Person of the Holy Spirit that was loosed to minister in and through that church.

The same power that raised Christ from the grave reached down to a man just walking by a church where God was moving. There were people inside who would love him. Waiting for him were an evangelist who is, and always was, a foot-washer who loves people right where they are; a Bible teacher who loves the Word of God, knows the power released when we act on that Word, and has a burden for the lost; an evangelist who has a passion for people to not only be saved, but to be delivered and set free from their past and all the darkness that has engulfed them, as well as the demons that torment them; and finally, a pastor who loves all people and is willing to do whatever it takes to see blind eyes open, broken hearts healed, and those in captivity set free. To God be the glory!

CHAPTER 25

YOU WILL ONLY KEEP WHAT YOU OBEY

I almost missed events like the one detailed in the previous chapter because I almost missed God by saying yes to becoming a Methodist minister. Let me be clear here. There is nothing wrong with becoming a Methodist minister. I have a high regard for many great Methodist pastors out there who are doing an outstanding job for the body of Christ. But when you know God has told you something else, you don't try to improve on God's word to you.

During my first year with Earl, the local district superintendent of the Methodist Conference called me to see if I would take a church. I told him I would pray about it and get in touch with him. Remember, God told me to minister with Earl two years. This was near the end of the first year; so as I prayed, the thought came to me that God was promoting me ahead of time. If I pastored a Methodist church, I would at least get a student's salary. Whatever it was, it was more than I would earn from Earl's ministry—nothing. The idea seemed good to me, so I told the superintendent that I would do it.

Earl and I had a week scheduled to minister in a church in Matthews, Virginia. We had been very busy, and I had already been away from home for about three weeks. So I called Mary Jane and asked her to take some time off and drive down to Matthews to be with us there, which she did. After Earl came back from jogging one afternoon, he said he heard a word from God which he thought might be for me. During his jog, he had been praying about our time together, knowing it was soon coming to an end because I had told the United Methodist district superintendent that I would take a church. Earl said he heard God say, "I will not give you more than you can handle, but you will only keep what you obey."

Today, I do not pretend to know all that God meant when He said that, but I did know at the time that I had a restlessness in my gut saying, "I told you to travel with Earl for two years." When this message came, I knew I had to obey what I had heard so I could keep what had been given. Yet, I did not want to travel another year. I wanted to stay home, and Mary Jane wanted me to stay home, too. She was there when we both heard this message, and we both knew we had to obey God and minister with Earl one more year. That night Earl preached and the hymn of invitation was, "I Surrender All." We went to the altar one more time to surrender our will to the Lord, and we pledged to continue on for the second year. Little did I know, my time with Earl would last almost a decade.

It was only at the beginning of the second year that the gift of teaching began to develop in me. We were in Statesboro, North Carolina, and Earl was not feeling well, so he asked me to teach the morning Bible study. God revealed His gift of teaching through me that day! When I was with Earl, he never taught another morning Bible study from that point on. I always did. The only time I would preach during the evening services, however, was when Earl was not feeling well, and that was not often!

CHAPTER 26

WHAT ARE YOU HEARING?

By now you may be thinking, I thought God said to minister for two years with Earl, and you traveled with him for ten?! He did say two; but during the time that I thought God was promoting me to become a Methodist preacher, I was not hearing anything from Him. I learned a valuable lesson. If you are not hearing from God, it most likely may be that you stopped obeying the last thing He told you to do. Go back and obey, and you will hear His voice again.

After the two years of ministry with Earl were up, I was asking God what was next. Again God seemed to be silent, so I continued to do what I had last heard God say. I decided that if I didn't hear something new, I would continue on the same course. Even though I did not travel every week with Earl, I ministered with him at least one or two weeks a month until 1991. During those ten years I also worked to build Eagle's Nest Family Campground and held Sunday services for the campers from Memorial Day through

Labor Day. I also taught weekly Bible studies on Saturday nights during the winter months. When I was away with Earl, Rick Betts would lead the studies, along with the worship. On most Saturday nights, we would have forty to fifty people in attendance.

During the last few years with Earl, I began to feel like we were spinning our wheels. We would have great meetings in churches and see God move to save, heal, and bring life back into a congregation—only to go back a couple of years later and notice that things had settled back to where they were before we arrived the first time. I began to pray and seek God about the main reason for this. As I observed, prayed, and asked questions, it became quite clear to me that the weak link was the failure of the pastor to provide leadership to continue the excitement and growth in his congregation.

I gradually realized that most churches would never grow above the spiritual level of their pastor. If you are a pastor, this is a scary statement; but it's one I believe to be true. I began to change my mind about many things. The first is that I now believe the local church is the foremost chosen vessel God chooses to use to bring change, salvation, and wholeness to our culture. I enjoyed going from church to church but clearly understood that if I wanted to see lasting fruit in the ministry, I had to stay planted in the local church and community to make a difference. I also knew that Jesus had said, "I will build my church and the gates of Hell will not prevail against it" (Matthew 16:18).

CHAPTER 27

THE BIRTH OF EAGLE'S NEST FELLOWSHIP

I thank God for every para-church organization, yet I firmly believe that they exist because the church has failed to perform the work that God has called it to. Eagle's Nest was first a para-church ministry. We ministered to campers during the summer and saw many of them receive salvation and get started on their spiritual journey, but those who failed to get connected to a local church have drifted away.

After I graduated from Bible school in 1981, many people wanted me to start a church. My response was always the same: "I don't want to start a church. I want to be a church. We don't need more churches; we just need to renew the ones we have. Stay where you are and make a difference there."

I had to eat some of those words. I am not sure I am qualified to define what a church is, but I know that a group of people meeting together every week, along with a sign over the door that says "ABC Church," does not make it a church.

We did a survey a few years ago and discovered that there are over two hundred and fifty churches in Sussex County, Delaware, and the average attendance is about forty people. Many of those churches had not received any new members through a profession of faith in years; that is, no one received salvation in the churches. Most growth, if they had any at all, was by transfer of membership. This confirmed what we had concluded many years prior to the survey. What was needed was a thriving church where the Word of God was taught with authority; where anyone could come regardless of how they looked and feel loved and accepted; where we could disciple them and equip them to give away what they had received; and where the body of Christ might grow and prosper.

Eagle's Nest Fellowship Church was about eight months old when Ernie Shepherd, who had been attending for a couple of months, came to me one Sunday morning and said, "I am so grateful for this church. I have been praying for this church for over two years." I replied that we had not been a church for that long. He said, "Oh, I didn't know the name of it. I just knew we needed a church where anyone could come and feel welcomed and loved." I knew then that we were on the right track!

As I reflect back on the eight additional years that I traveled with Earl and the actual planting of the church, I can see that God was preparing me, as well as many other people, to birth a new church in Sussex County. There may be other churches that began as we did, but I am not aware of them. We established a church to fill a void, not because of a split or division between individuals. It wasn't that we were angry with anyone; we just didn't want church people to come because our focus was on the unsaved and unchurched in Sussex County, Delaware. (They still did, anyway.)

When we birthed the church, over eighty percent of the population of the county was unchurched, according to our research. This means that about one hundred and twenty thousand people in Sussex County did not attend church. The eighty percent figure coincides with the national average, according to George Barna, the national church pollster. After looking at this information, talking to people, and praying, I modified my earlier opinion that we didn't need another church in the county. I decided we needed more churches that take the Word of God seriously and are committed to making disciples, not just converts. It appears that too many churches are just looking for attendees, merely content to survive.

After ten years of full-time ministry with Earl, I saw firsthand that the body of Christ had failed to fulfill Ephesians 4, which refers to fully operating in all five of the offices that Jesus left for the church: preacher, teacher, apostle, prophet and evangelist. Ephesians 4:12 says clearly that ministers with these gifts should equip the saints for the work of ministry. For too long the church has acted like the pastors, teachers, apostles, prophets, and evangelists should do all the work. In fact, in most cases, the church expects the pastor to do all the work, while the other four offices are optional.

The failure of the church to use its greatest asset, the lay people, to do the work of the ministry is the major reason so little gets accomplished for the Kingdom. The local church must do a better job of equipping people to do the work of the ministry.

In the summer of 1991, I began to sense in my spirit that we should stop having the Bible study each Saturday night. We took a break each summer anyway between Memorial Day and Labor Day, when we led the Sunday morning services for the campers. I just knew, though, that we were not supposed to start up again in the fall. God wanted to do something new.

Eagle's Nest Fellowship Church began in September of 1991 when I announced that we were going to continue to have services each Sunday. Notice that I did not say we were going to start a church; I said that we were going to continue Sunday services. I told the people there that if they didn't already have a home church, we would be honored to have them come and worship with us. I had already talked to Rick Betts and he agreed to officially become our praise and worship leader.

I also received much encouragement from Dale Mast, pastor of the Jireh Christian Center, now Destiny Worship Center, in Dover, Delaware. Pastor Dale and I co-hosted a weekly call-in talk show, "The Word Became Flesh," on WXPZ, the local Christian radio station. We were able to minister to many people over the phone as we talked about many topical issues from biblical perspectives. Dale kept saying to me, "You already are a church. You just meet on Saturday nights instead of Sunday mornings."

The Sunday after Labor Day, 1991, we met at the campground for our very first service. Thirty-three people showed up that morning. The following Sunday, we met in the basement of our home due to inclement weather, and about fifty people attended.

The Clyde Betts & Son Hardware Store had closed its doors for business and was sitting empty, so we soon began to rent that facility when our basement was bursting at the seams. The people continued to come, and we were enjoying fellowship, ministry, and praise and worship at a whole new level.

After we officially became a church that was meeting at the hardware store, the week-to-week excitement was contagious. We grew so rapidly that all the staff could do was react. Not much planning was involved, but it sure was exciting! New people came every week. People were getting saved on a regular basis, and the ministry was unbelievable. The praise and worship under Rick's leadership was awesome. In all our years that we ministered together, we never shared with each other what sermons I would preach or what songs he would select for the services, but they always seemed to flow together and fit like a hand and glove.

Since we didn't know how to structure a church and the New Testament was silent on how it should be done, we continued on as it seemed good to us. We already had a 501(c)(3) tax-exempt status for the campground under the name of Eagle's Nest Ministries. We had a legal corporate board of three people and an active board of twelve people. It seemed like a good number to me; after all, Jesus picked twelve men to be His disciples. As the thirteenth member of the board, I thought that I could break any tie votes if they occurred. Little did I know how soon that would occur!

We experienced strong, steady growth during our first year, averaging about one hundred and twenty-five attendees each week. In the midst of this, the owners of the building where we held our meetings needed to sell the property and offered it to us before they listed it on the market. We had a dream, a vision, momentum, and one hundred and twenty-five attendees—but no money. We had a board meeting, and I presented the plan to buy the property. After much discussion, we took a vote. Six voted to buy the building, and the other six voted against it. Because of the momentum we had, I knew that we needed the property for many important reasons. For one, there was no other place to meet in our area that could handle one hundred and twenty-five adults, with room for growth and a place for children to be ministered to as well. I broke the tie vote, and we made plans to purchase the property. The next hurdle was to find the money we needed.

After being turned down by two banks, I was discouraged. Then we found County Bank, who believed in our vision and loaned us the money. Eight years later, when our attendance was about eight hundred and we were looking for money to build our new facility, several banks called us, wanting to loan our church the money. At the time, we were still using County Bank, who believed in us, and we appreciated this. Needless to say, we stuck with them.

Looking back on the decision to purchase the Clyde Betts property, I learned a few things, namely, that voting always tends to divide one faction against another. A few years later I had another opportunity to vote. In 1992, WXPZ began an outreach ministry to the area called LambJam. This was a contemporary Christian music festival that also featured teaching, fellowship, and evangelistic events, similar to Fishnet in Virginia and Creation in Pennsylvania.

We had all the ingredients to make it happen. The radio station coordinated the festival, booking the artists and advertising the event. Eagle's Nest Family Campground provided the perfect location, and several people who had been on staff at Fishnet came and helped our staff during the festival. LambJam featured some of the top names in contemporary and Christian rock music, which attracted thousands of people to Milton, Delaware, every year. The average attendance was about four thousand; however, one year when Carman (at the peak of his career) was the headliner, ten thousand people attended the final night of the festival.

Because of LambJam, we ended up owning the property that now includes the church, school, and gymnasium on it. The land we previously owned and operated for the campground quickly proved to be too small for the LambJam event. So, I approached the owners of the property next to us to see if we could rent or lease about five acres of land from them for a parking area. They did not want to set aside five acres for us; instead, they said that the campground should buy it. I responded that even though the campground was as big as we could handle at that time, I would like to own the property to build a church on it someday. The owner then told me that he decided to cancel his plans to develop it and would sell the property to us. I told him, however, that there was a major reason the church could not buy it. We did not have any money; besides, we still were paying off a mortgage on the hardware store property.

The owner of the land called a few days later and offered to sell us fifty-seven acres and hold the mortgage on the property. He listed the terms, and I knew it was doable. He wanted twenty thousand dollars down and the same amount annually over a five-year period with a balloon payment at the end, along with interest paid quarterly. I was excited. I knew we could do this and that God was giving us a chance to invest in the future. I presented this proposal to our advisory board and opened it up for discussion. The first comment was, "We don't need 57 acres of land; we just need a decent building to meet in." This was true. We already had people calling us, "the Branch Davidian Compound." Our current facilities were in poor condition. They consisted of a hodgepodge of old buildings which had once housed a hardware store, egg-grading facility, farm shop and feed/grain warehouse. This was not all bad. We knew that those who attended our services were not coming for the facilities. We liked to think of the buildings as rustic.

A CONSENSUS

After some other comments made at the board meeting, I remembered the last discussion about purchasing the hardware store. I did not want to be the tiebreaker regarding a $300,000 loan to purchase land. I wanted all the board to know that this either was God or was not God, so I stopped the discussion and announced that we would go on a weekend retreat and do nothing but get alone with God, pray, and seek a consensus.

At the retreat, the board member who first voiced opposition to the purchase came back to me and said, "I believe this is God. We need to think about the future and make some long-range plans." One by one, they all came forward and said something very similar to me. We unanimously made the decision to purchase the fifty-seven acres and announced to the congregation that we needed $20,000 to begin the process. It took less than two weeks to raise the money, and no individual gift was larger than $1000.

We were off and running. We paid the entire $300,000 off in about three years, and then started to make plans to build. We had a weekly attendance of about four hundred people, so it was a major decision to determine how big of a facility was big enough.

To this day, I still do not like voting. I am a firm believer that we need less voting and more praying that God would lead us.

GOD WANTS TO USE PEOPLE

During this time we also started a Christian daycare. I felt like God was not only steering me toward starting a daycare facility with Christian principles that would become a bridge to a Christian school, but He was also telling me who should be in charge of it. I had known Lucy Dutton as a casual acquaintance for years, but never thought about her regarding Eagle's Nest. Lucy had a small home daycare; but when I approached her about doing that on a larger scale, she was not interested. Others knew about my vision and approached me about helping manage the daycare. I said no to all of them because I felt that God had said Lucy was the one. God was the one who chose Lucy, not me. It was over a year later when God changed Lucy's heart, and she called me to accept the job.

Lucy is a great example of how God has sent key people to be "Aaron and Hur" to me (Exodus 17:10-13). These people were committed to God, and He let them see the vision He has for

Eagle's Nest. Most of these precious people are gifted in areas I am not. It's the only way a church that began with thirty-three attendees could, in a few short years, grow to have a paid staff of over a hundred people.

God wants to use people to change our world. He is still using people, not just those who are especially gifted or possess supernatural abilities, but ones like you and me who are available for what He wants to do. People ask me all the time about how God speaks to me. I can use Lucy as one example of how God speaks and leads me. With Lucy, there was a knowing, not an audible voice or even a leading. It was just a knowing in my knower that she was the one to begin the daycare ministry.

Lucy is still working in that capacity, also functioning as our school administrator. She has grown with us and is a blessing to the ministry. God has sent so many others to this ministry who have a special place in my heart.

Sonny Reed, a high school classmate who has became a close friend over the years, left a very good secular job to join our ministry at a tremendous personal sacrifice to him and his family to obey what we both believed God was leading us to do. Sonny came on staff as the church administrator and took quite a load off of me. I have a habit of wanting to do it myself, and having someone on staff with me whom I know has no agenda but to obey God and help me to reach people for Jesus is quite a blessing. Thank you, Sonny.

GOD'S FAVOR

Earlier I mentioned that I believe God has a purpose, a plan, and a place for all of us to minister. I am sure that the place is of special importance. When God gifts people to fulfill His purpose and plan for their lives, I also believe in my life, as well as in the lives of others, that the right place will afford us favor. We will have God's favor when we are in the right place, but we will experience less favor when we are in the wrong place.

God's gifts and passions will work anywhere, but we all need His favor to make a major impact for Him. In other words, you can have all the right stuff, but be in the wrong place. Jesus Himself could not do mighty works in His hometown because the people only knew him as Joseph and Mary's son, a carpenter.

I started a church and ministry in my hometown. The reasons, I think, are mostly because people knew me B.C.: "Before Christ" changed me. I think that was true with Jesus, as well as all of us. We all know a few horror stories about hot-shot Elmer Gantry types coming to town and making a lot of noise, but producing no lasting fruit. During our first service, I said, "I am home. I am not going anywhere; I will be here for the long haul. We will enjoy what God will do through us, or we will be here to pick up the pieces of what fails. I'm here."

Much of the success we have enjoyed has been because we have found favor with people in our area. As I studied the Bible, I kept reading about many of the saints of God, as well as Jesus, who went forth and found favor with God and man (Luke 2:52). I believe that God intends for all of us to increase in wisdom along with stature, and to find favor with both God and man. I think the amount of favor we find with men is dependent upon us being in the right place. Let me explain how this works.

As I mentioned in a previous chapter, in the early days of the ministry, God used me as a vessel to bring healing to broken people whose marriages were in trouble. I never asked to do this because I never felt called or qualified to do this. They just came, and I responded to Jesus. It never mattered to me where they went to church, or even if they went to church. I just knew that all of them had a spiritual problem, not a marriage problem. As I reflect back on the years, I know that a lot of the favor we received was due to the fruit produced in many marriages. People in the area who have never worshiped with us at Eagle's Nest still have a favorable opinion of us.

One of the early couples whom I ministered to was a couple from Milford, Delaware, who came to see me through the invitation of a friend who attended Eagle's Nest. The wife had been married twice before marrying her current husband, and he had also been married before. They both told me later that they really came to me just to get their friend off their case.

At the first session with them, I told them that neither God nor I could heal their marriage because their marriage was not the problem. They were the real problem. I explained to them how God heals people, not marriages. Healed people produce healed marriages, so if they were both willing to give Jesus control of their lives, their marriage would be healed. Years later when they gave a public testimony about this event, the wife confessed that she said to him as they were getting in their car, "This guy is crazy! We came to him with our marriage going to hell, and he wants to talk to us about Jesus. What has Jesus got to do with anything?" They later began to understand as they walked in the Kingdom ways.

Favor was proven when we made plans to build our new family worship center, a facility that was state of the art and could seat one thousand people. When we started making plans, we were still meeting in the old hardware store building, holding multiple services. The church office was in our home and my wife, Mary Jane, did all the administrative work for the four hundred attendees of the church, as well as the campground and daycare.

As we started our very first building campaign, we were amazed by those who participated. The first large gift came when a couple who was getting ready to move out of the state asked me how close we were to building the worship center. I replied that we were about $150,000 short of even giving serious thought to beginning. The following week, they waited after the service to tell me that they wanted to give the full amount so we could get started, even though they were moving out of state and would not get to worship with us in the new facility. That's favor!

After construction began, we also began to enjoy more favor. Much of it came through donated labor but also in donated materials. Over $250,000, a quarter of a million dollars, was given by people who do not attend Eagle's Nest. Most churches talk about how stressful building campaigns are, but we did not find it to be so at all. It was an exciting time for all of us as we marveled at how God works. Let me share one more money-related miracle that is recent.

The construction project at Eagle's Nest was ultimately broken down into three phases. We called the family worship center, Phase I, and the school, Phase II. The gymnasium, which we dedicated in January of 2007, was Phase III of our long-range plans.

As the school grew (the 2008 enrollment was over four hundred and twenty-five pre K-8 students), so did the cost of materials and services for Phase III. Every school needs a gym, especially if you have junior high students. The real challenge for the administration was how to pay for it. The gym, unlike more classrooms, did not allow us to add more students to generate more income. These monies had to come from other sources. When we started talking about a gym, we thought we could build it for $1,000,000. While we were getting proposal bids for construction, we discovered that the new gym would actually cost $3,000,000.

As we were praying and agonizing over this number, we really did not know what to do. The church had underwritten the school since its inception and also built the new sixteen classrooms for it (Phase II). The resources were not there for a gym costing $3,000,000. Most of our parents struggled to pay the tuition, so we felt that increasing the cost of tuition was not an option.

Again the favor of God came into play. A man who had never been to Eagle's Nest Church, School, or Campground, but one whom I had personally found favor with, walked into my office one day. I had developed a friendship with this man through our mutual love of the outdoors and hunting. I would describe him as a seeker, one looking for answers. I was expecting him since we were going to lunch together, but I wasn't expecting what happened next as he handed me a check for $1,000,000 and said, "Use this however it's needed."

My response surprised me almost as much as it did him. I handed it back to him and said, "Let me talk to you about something that means more to me than that check." We talked about his salvation, and he prayed the sinner's prayer with me. He gave me the check back, and we both rejoiced. This was favor, both with God and man.

Five days later, a friend of his who knew about this event mailed me a check matching that amount in gratitude for what God was doing in his friend's life. To God be the glory! Nothing beats favor with God and man!

SEEKER-SENSITIVE

Much has been spoken and written about the seeker-sensitive movement. Many people criticize the concept, believing that type of worship service disrespects the Holy Spirit. I would agree that we must never dilute the gospel; however, we must be sensitive to those who are actively seeking something. Usually they don't know what they are seeking. We want them to experience something that will make them come back. It's hard to minister to an empty pew.

In the early days of Eagle's Nest Fellowship Church, one of our identifying characteristics was the effective use of prayer circles. We had always wanted to provide an avenue for people to be prayed for in our services, so in the beginning we just asked people to stand and share any requests. The pastor would receive the request and pray after everyone had a chance to make their petitions known. This worked fine until we had over one hundred and fifty people in attendance and it started taking a large amount of time out of the service. We wanted to keep prayer an integral part of our service; however, we didn't want to shortchange the time allotted for the message.

While attending a Jack Hayford conference, I heard Pastor Hayford address that very issue. He said that was why his church, The Church on The Way in Van Nuys, California, had started doing prayer circles. People were asked to stand and form circles of six to eight people. They would introduce themselves by their first names, and anyone could ask for prayer. Despite some initial resistance, we started using the prayer circle concept at Eagle's Nest. After the shock wore off, most people began to enjoy it. They were almost like mini small-group meetings during church. We continued to have these ministry groups for years.

After moving into our new facility, we were enjoying about twelve to fifteen first-time guests each week. I sometimes wondered where they all came from. Unfortunately, a large percentage of these visitors did not return.

We polled these people and asked them why they did not return. We learned that they found our church friendly and welcoming. They enjoyed the praise and worship and got a lot out of the message, but the prayer circles made them uncomfortable. We began to prayerfully consider what to do. We wanted people to come back. We had to ask ourselves for whom we were doing these circles—us or the guests? We decided to stop the circles and received a lot of criticism for it from some of the folks who had been with us from the beginning.

Our decision was made in consideration to the feelings of our visitors. The prayer circles were effective for our regulars; however, if we were frightening the seekers or new believers and they did not come back, how could we ever grow or reach out? We felt that the mature believers had other alternatives for prayer circles, including our church-sponsored small group meetings.

Church members must be free to be themselves, but at the same time, they must be careful not to frighten the seekers who come to the services by their words or actions. Where should we draw the line? I don't know, but when the fundamentalists tell me that our church is too wild and the Pentecostals tell me we are too dead, I feel like we are about where we should be. To those who disagree with all this, I tell them to come and see. We will make you feel welcome, love and pray for you, and help you experience the fullness of Christ in your life.

In August of 1999, the dream became a reality. We held our very first worship service in a packed sanctuary on Sunday morning. We broadcast it live on the Internet (at the time, a very cutting-edge technology), and we felt like we were in heaven. As I stood in the pulpit that first service, I was overwhelmed by the size of the sanctuary and the excitement of the place. Earl Tyson, Dr. Ken Stewart (from Rhema), and John Hobbs came to help us celebrate and dedicate our new facility. I have already shared stories about Earl and Dr. Stewart. The other man who has had a great impact on my life is John Hobbs from Wilmington, North Carolina.

JOHN

I first met John through Earl Tyson's brother, Bobby. Bobby had traveled with John for a season. John has a way of preaching that just seems to draw everyone in. His Southern drawl and charm allows him to say things to people that I could never say, such as, "Get your hips over here!" John, who grew up without a father, can enable people to experience the Father's love and heart like no other person I know. Only God can do this for a man who was fatherless. John is a great communicator who exudes the love of Jesus from every fiber of his being. John is real. What you see in the pulpit is what you see on the street. When you go to dinner with him, I can assure you that he will talk to someone about the Lord before you leave the place.

John visited us one winter while we were vacationing in Florida. One morning during breakfast, he got into a conversation with the waitress at Perkins Pancake House. She shared about her life and the struggles she was having. She did this after John had talked about Jesus with her. Before we left the restaurant, I saw John put a large bill into her hand. That's how John Hobbs is. John is a friend, a peer, and a mentor. John is a minister to ministers, and he has influenced this ministry greatly. His son, Scott, is currently the worship pastor at Eagle's Nest.

CHAPTER 33

STEWARDS

After the completion of the new family worship center, it seemed as though the next step was to multiply ourselves. During this time, I was amazed by how often God would talk about multiplying. The pattern for this is established in Genesis 1:28 when God said, "Be fruitful and multiply." God has not changed His mind. He still wants fruit to be produced in our lives (John 15) and for us to multiply in every area of our lives.

In the parable of the talents, to those who multiplied, He said, "Well done, thou good and faithful servant, enter into the joy of the Lord." He called the one who did not multiply "lazy and wicked." There are two important lessons in this parable that should change how the church and Christians act. The first is that the goods or talents which were given belonged to the owner, not to those who had received them. It is imperative for the Christian community to understand that all we have is His. We don't own anything; we are simply stewards, or managers, of the resources that He has given us. It makes such a difference when we know we don't own anything but that everything belongs to Him. He alone is the One who has given us ALL that we have, whether it is a little or much. It's all His. That is so liberating and powerful that it makes such a difference in how we handle material goods and talents.

One of the most valuable lessons I ever taught concerning this I learned from John Maxwell. I borrowed his concept later as I was trying to communicate the principle of stewardship. During the message, I stopped and announced that I was a little short for the week, so I asked if could anyone could give me a hundred dollars. Chuck Tribbitt, a member of the congregation, immediately ran up on the platform and gave me that amount. I said thanks and proceeded with the morning message.

I could tell that the congregation stopped hearing me when Chuck came up. Ten or fifteen minutes later, I finally came back to the issue of the hundred dollars. I explained that the reason Chuck was so eager to give me the cash was because it wasn't his money. (I had arranged with Chuck to help me by giving him the money before the service.)

When we surrender ownership of all of our stuff as well as our spouse, children, and money and appreciate them and receive them as God's gifts to us, they become more meaningful to us. I appreciate that God has allowed Mary Jane to share her life with me. I don't own her, and she knows she doesn't own me; but the journey He has allowed us to travel together has been such a blessing to us, and I pray a blessing to many others.

The second lesson is that God is not at all pleased if we don't use what He has entrusted to us and multiply it—not add to it, but multiply it. Because of this, we knew that the eighty percent of Sussex County who did not go to church needed a location within thirty minutes of their home. We realized that we were not the only Christ-centered, Bible-preaching, disciple-making church in the area. There were many good ones, but being biased, we wanted everyone to be exposed to the Eagle's Nest experience. We began to make plans to provide a meeting place on the western side of the county. About two hundred people from that area were driving to Milton to attend church each week. We asked Rick Betts to be the pastor of what was originally Eagle's Nest West, now fully autonomous as Crossroads Community Church, and let God multiply on the other side of the county.

MISSIONS

During our early years of growth, we helped many missionaries in several locations. I have always felt that I wanted to help individual people rather than focus on ministries. So even though we support ministries, we invest in people whom we know are under their authority.

Before he entered the ministry, Carl Vincent owned the farm where the church and campground are now located. He left the farm and attended Bible college in Pensacola, Florida. At Pensacola he received his call to the pastorate, later becoming pastor of Liberty North East in Pensacola as an associate of Ken Summeral.

During a missions trip to Russia, Carl felt that God was leading him to minister there on a full-time basis. The board and elders at his church confirmed this call, so he and his wife packed up and spent a total of seven years ministering in Russia. The last three were spent in Siberia. (I have a picture of Carl and his late wife,

Phyllis, standing under a bank thermometer that read thirty degrees below zero.)

Because we knew Carl and Phyllis, we wanted to help them in their ministry. Eagle's Nest included them in the missions outreach program and supported them monthly. When Carl knew that his call to Russia was over, he stopped in Delaware to visit on his way to Florida. I talked to him about joining our staff at Eagle's Nest. After much prayer, he came on staff as teaching pastor and added so much to our church. He was another of God's gifts to help all of us.

SMALL-GROUP MINISTRY

Carl introduced us to the Principle of 12, a small-group ministry which I believe is one of the most biblical of all of the small-group ministries out there. I am firmly convinced that it is impossible to grow an effective large church without small groups.

After visiting Bethany World Prayer Center in Baton Rouge, Louisiana, pastored by Larry Stockstill, we were convinced that this was what would work for us. As of this writing, we are still adjusting and learning how to do the Principle of 12 effectively. The failures have occurred because we have not followed the principles exactly. The key is to train leaders who can see the vision with you. Each small-group leader, in essence, becomes a pastor to the twelve in their group, and during the growth period raises up a helper who will launch a new group when the existing group exceeds fourteen or fifteen people.

It all begins with the senior pastor leading his own group of twelve from the staff, and each staff member has his own group of twelve as well. This requires a high level of commitment, so other programs may have to be eliminated to cut down on meetings.

I believe the plan of Jesus is to train disciples. The Principle of 12 raises up leaders who, in turn, raise up other leaders. It is the greatest way I know to fulfill Ephesians 4.

CHAPTER 36

MAKING DISCIPLES

During one of our services in the Midwest, a lady who had been a faithful attendee and member of the local Methodist church came up to Earl after a service and said, "Isn't it a shame that Jesus died so young? Think of all the good He could have done if He had lived until He was seventy-five."

My fear is that this woman is not alone in misunderstanding what it was Jesus came to do. Jesus came to not only pay our sin debt for us, but He also came to empower us to do the work of the ministry that He did (John 14:12). As the church universal, we must therefore do a better job of making disciples.

At another church during Holy Week, Earl had preached a great message on the power of the cross. During the fellowship time after the service, a man who had also been in the church a long time came up to Earl and said, "Earl, that was a great message on the cross, but I have a question for you. Do I have to believe that Jesus died for me? I've been good all my life." How sad! This is just one example of how poorly the church is doing at making disciples.

CHAPTER 37

MESSIAH'S VINEYARD

The addition of Carl Vincent to our staff was such a blessing to everyone but especially to me. He knew that God sent him specifically to help me. Carl is one of the finest Bible teachers I have ever heard. He is a man of great integrity and character who teaches and preaches with passion and lives out his faith on a daily basis.

As we were beginning to prepare for my retirement from Eagle's Nest, and after his beloved Phyllis passed away at an early age, Carl told me it was time for him to go and do something different. Because I was so close to Carl, I had difficulty believing that this was God. As I prayed, however, I knew that it was God and he needed to follow Him, even though I did not want him to leave. We were grateful for all that Carl had accomplished over the five years with us, and we helped him in a small way to begin a new work in Laurel, Delaware, called Messiah's Vineyard. God is blessing him there.

When Eagle's Nest Fellowship Church was birthed in 1991, I was celebrating my fifty-fourth birthday. It seems as though I was a late starter in everything I had ever done. Me? Pioneer a new church at age fifty-four? Was I crazy? I don't believe that at all. I believe I was obedient. There have been times when I thought about how much more I could have accomplished if I had started the church at age twenty-five, but I quickly dismissed those thoughts, knowing that God's plans for my life are perfect. I suppose that I could have regrets about being so old when I got saved, but even that is foolishness because I think that God has used all my experiences—failures, successes, and everything in between—to make me who I am today. You may argue with what God has done through me, but in spite of me, God has touched many people through this ministry. As I write this, an event that happened many years ago comes to mind.

Earl and I were leading a week of services in North Central Iowa. As I was teaching the Bible study, a lady who had been a faithful attendee all week wanted to know if I would come and see her husband, who was unsaved. He had suffered two heart attacks, was about seventy-five years old, and she wanted him to accept the Lord. He was a retired hog farmer, so she thought I might be able to reach him. I visited their home that afternoon. After talking about hog farming for a while, we talked about Jesus and salvation.

After I had explained the plan of salvation to him, he asked me, "If I pray with you, does that mean I have to go to church?" I replied, "No. This prayer, if you really mean what I am asking you to pray, will guarantee that you will go to heaven, not to church."

I could see that he was relieved, so I then added, "But let me warn you, if you pray this prayer from your heart, you probably will want to go to church." He prayed the prayer, and after rejoicing with him, I asked, "Why are you so concerned about going to church?"

He replied that he had agoraphobia, which resulted in severe anxiety or panic attacks when he was in a crowd of people. I then asked him if he would let me pray for Jesus to heal this disorder, and with his permission I prayed for him to be healed in Jesus' name.

At the service that night, after Earl preached and gave the invitation, I went to the altar to minister to the people who came. Amazingly, my new farmer friend was one of the people down front asking for prayer. Knowing he had just received Christ that afternoon, I asked him, "Why did you come forward? Can I pray for you about something?" With tears running down his cheeks, he said, "Son, I just want to thank you for all you have done for me and my family. I have been healed of my disorder. I have been in this service tonight and all is well." We knelt at the altar together and prayed and cried, all because God used one pig farmer to help another pig farmer find healing through Jesus.

Several years later I was having a bad day. Truthfully, I was having a pity party for myself, wondering if anything I had ever done had made an eternal consequence in anyone's life.

When I went to the mailbox, there was God's answer waiting for me. It was a letter from that Iowa pig farmer's wife, letting me know that he had died a few weeks earlier. She went on to update me on the events of their lives after our visit in their church. She said the change in him was drastic. After his healing, he went to church regularly with her and would talk about Jesus at the drop of a hat. She also said that before our visit, he and his son had a broken relationship; so they had not talked in years. She went on to share that the relationship had been restored and he died in peace with God and his family. She wanted to thank me for coming to their church and to their home. Praise God!

TRANSFERRING THE MANTLE

Starting a church at age fifty-four, when many people are thinking about their retirement, required me to start thinking about a succession plan for the ministry. I knew that I needed to make plans to mentor a younger man and transfer the mantle to him when God was ready. After several years of ministry, I felt as though God was telling me to transfer at age seventy, so I promised Him and myself that I would get out of the way at age seventy. This was a most difficult transition for me. I don't feel as though God is done with me, but I know the church needs young leadership. I also know they need mentoring because there are some things that only come through experience.

On January 1, 2001, I hired a younger man to be our youth pastor, knowing he was not really a youth pastor at heart. Bob Weed had been the senior pastor of Delmar Christian Center in Delmar, Delaware, and he had a vision for Sussex County.

Bob came on staff, and he and his wife, Patti, have been a blessing to Eagle's Nest Fellowship Church. Bob has grown and is growing with the church, and I believe he is God's choice to lead us into the next level of church growth. Bob is a good teacher and preacher, and he has a great handle on the Word of God. I am grateful for Bob, Patti, and their two sons, Kyle and Caleb, and am looking forward to being there for him in the years ahead.

THE VISION CONTINUES . . .

I officially retired at the end of December in 2006. Mary Jane and I then took a three-month vacation to write this book and seek God about what is next for our lives. I truly believe that God is transitioning me to the next phase of my life. I don't pretend to know all of what that is, but in addition to just being there for Bob and the staff of Eagle's Nest, I know that our desire to build a continuous-care community on our property for senior citizens (fifty-five years of age and older) is God's plan for us. We've checked the demographics of who is moving into the area, and most are at, or near, retirement age. Some are fully retired. Others are semi-retired: that is, they need to (and/or want to) work on a part-time basis. As these people age, the need for retirement communities, assisted living facilities, and nursing care homes will increase.

God has blessed us with over one hundred and fifty acres to be used for Him. How will we do this? I don't know, but I firmly believe that God will send the people and the resources to make it happen. Just before I began to write this book, I asked someone to pray for me because I did not know how to write a book. They responded, "Did you know how to start a church before you began?" Even though I was late in life getting started in my spiritual journey, I now look back and see how God was working through all the events to make this happen in my life. To God be the glory for all He has done!

CHAPTER 40

CALLED BY GOD

When we started the church, my past experience in church was pretty poor. I never had the opportunity to sit under a pastor who had the vision and passion to build a church. Most denominations have a structure that encourages mediocrity, and the majority of their pastors just don't want to rock the boat by being too liberal or too conservative. Their desire is to stay calm and hopefully get promoted to a bigger church with a bigger salary, instead of trying to build one where they are. There are exceptions, but generally all this is true.

There are great churches in every denomination, and I have visited many of them. I have been in six of the top ten largest and fastest-growing churches in America. The one thing they all have in common is a pastor who communicates well, has a vision for his community that is much larger than his church, and knows he is there for the long haul. He is not looking for a promotion; instead, he is looking for the Kingdom to come in and through the church.

Too many pastors feel like hirelings because that is how they are treated. In so many words and attitudes, their board members tell them, "Preacher, if you don't do this like we want, we will replace you. We were here when you got here, and we will be here when you are gone."

I have searched through the Bible, and I can't find any verse that says the people should decide what and how the preacher should minister. Whatever happened to the concept of a person called by God into the ministry? When God sends you, you tend to be less intimidated by the people. You cannot simply acquiesce to the wishes of the congregation and be successful; instead, you must respond to what God desires for the church.

CHAPTER 41

PRAYER WARRIORS

We must never forget that the church is God's idea, and He just lets us join in with Him. Pastors must stop trying to please the people and rather just focus on pleasing God. When I do that, it has been my experience that more people are pleased with me. I really believe that God spoke to me early on about the two groups of people in the church that I should never listen to. One group is my critics, because I am not as bad as they think I am. The other is my fan club, because I am not as good as they think I am. Thank God for both groups. I can learn from both groups, but I always count on a team of prayer warriors to lift me before the throne every day.

Whenever we travel south, I try to visit a lady who celebrated her hundredth birthday in 2006. She and her family moved out of state a couple of years ago. Before she left, she told me she had prayed for me without fail every day for twelve years. Grace

Dibble is a Proverbs 31 woman if I've ever met one. The wife of a pastor who has gone on to glory, she is a true saint of God who is also a prayer warrior. I am convinced that every day when she wakes up, the Devil cries, "Oh no, she's awake again!"

CHAPTER 42

THROUGH THE SHADOW

Whether we are one hundred or ten years old, we all must be fully prepared to die before we are truly prepared to live. Death still creates much fear in the lives of most people because we really don't understand the biblical principles of death.

You may recall the Midwest farm crisis in the 1980s. Land prices and crop prices declined as interest rates soared. Many farmers lost their farms, and they were committing suicide at an alarming rate. During that crisis, Earl and I spent some time ministering in Iowa.

I learned a couple of spiritual truths during that time. The first had to do with death. I had just read the 23rd Psalm and then went jogging, which I was doing at the time on a regular basis. As I went around a bend of the gravel road, there was a large black walnut tree at the edge of the pasture, next to the fence. The sun behind the tree was casting a large shadow down the road where I was jogging. As I continued on around the bend and through the shadow, I heard in my spirit these words, "That is what death is to the Christian. It is but a shadow, and there is no substance to it." I then recalled the words of David in Psalm 23: "Yea, though I walk through the valley of the shadow of death, I shall fear no evil."

I believe that God was giving me a glimpse of what death is like—no substance. I could not jog through the black walnut tree, but I could jog through the shadow of the black walnut tree. This fueled my desire to discover all that I could about this feared subject. During this time Earl and I stopped to visit his Aunt Pauline in North Carolina. Earl couldn't wait to get there. Earl loved to eat, and Aunt Pauline loved to cook. Boy, could she cook!

Aunt Pauline was also the unofficial Tyson historian. She seemed to know details about each family member. After dinner, the discussion turned to the death of Earl's younger brother, George. Earl shared the events of his last night in the hospital when all the Tyson brothers, five in all, were in the room where George was dying. George suddenly woke up and told them, "I have just seen Momma, Daddy, and Uncle App. They said they are anxiously awaiting my arrival, and I am going on to be with them."

George closed his eyes, and in a short time he was dead. Aunt Pauline was shocked when Earl shared whom George had seen. She said, "Earl, how did George know Uncle App? App died when George was a baby. He never knew him." In a few minutes Aunt Pauline said, "Earl, George saw the same people who were in the birthing room the night he was born!" We suddenly realized that those who were present when George was born into this world were the same ones who were there to welcome him into the next. They were part of his heavenly host welcoming him into a higher dimension of life.

CHAPTER 43

A HIGHER DIMENSION

I began to see the similarity between birth and death. Each one transitions us into a higher dimension of life. I believe that God intended for each of these events to be a blessing, as well as a bonding time for all involved. Back in 1957 when our son, Bill Jr., was born, the nurses made me leave the room during the delivery and go down the hall to a waiting room, as though I had the measles or something. Now we understand the value of the bonding time when all members of the family can be present in the birthing room as something miraculous in the spirit realm happens. This, I believe, is what God wants to happen.

As I mentioned previously, I lost my father when I was only seventeen years old. Dad was only forty-nine. They treated him for indigestion for about a week. On Sunday he suffered another attack and was rushed to the hospital where the doctors diagnosed the problem to be his heart. Late in the afternoon, they gave Mom a sedative so she could rest. I was alone with him in the room when he had another attack. I rushed to get the doctor; but they would not let me back in the room, so he died alone.

Since becoming a pastor, I have spent many hours with families who have lost loved ones. There is something special about going on to glory surrounded by people whom you love and who love you. In our lifetime, a hospice program enables the sick to remain at home and depart surrounded by loved ones. Death, like birth, is truly a spiritual event.

If you could talk to a baby in the womb just before delivery, he would probably say something like this: "I don't want to go. I've not done this before. It's scary and I don't understand it." From the vantage point of the womb, the birthing process looks like death to the baby. What it actually involves is a transition from the womb to a higher dimension of life into this world. It's good for the baby, as well as for the mother. There has to be a birth for the good of each.

Death is the same. To those of us who are in Christ, death is a transition to a higher dimension of life. It is not a cessation of anything but a transition to something higher and better than we have ever had before. The word death means "to be separated from." In Genesis, spiritual death occurred when man disobeyed God. In other words, he was separated from God.

In physical death, we are separated from our bodies, but we still have our spirits and souls. Read the story Jesus told about Lazarus and the rich man: both had died (Luke 16:19-31). Death should not be frightening to us as Christians because we have the assurance that we are moving to a higher realm to spend eternity with Jesus. It is sad for those left behind, but glorious for the one moving on. For the Christian, death is just a shadow.

CHAPTER 44

WHAT IS YOUR IDENTITY?

The other spiritual truth I saw clearly that year in Iowa was about identity. All of us, whether we are conscious of it or not, have an identity. We see ourselves in a certain way.

As we ministered to those farmers in Iowa, I began to see a common thread that ran throughout the farm community. As I explored this, I began to realize how people got their identity. Most people find their identity in what they do. If you ask a hundred people who they are, ninety-nine will tell you what they do: "I am a farmer, a doctor, a lawyer, or even a pastor." What we do, however, is not who we truly are.

One of the dangers of finding our identity in what we do is that if we lose what we do or no longer can perform our vocation, we have lost our identity, or who we are. If you are a farmer and lose the farm that perhaps your dad or grandpa farmed, you really feel like a failure. You have lost not only what you do, but also the land to do it on; therefore, the Devil will tell you, "You are a failure, so you should just die. Everybody will be better off."

Nothing is further from the truth. If we fail to find our identity in God, we will at some point think we are a failure. We must rather agree with Him. I am who God says I am, whether I feel like it or not. When tempted in the wilderness, Jesus said to the Devil, "Man does not live by bread alone." In this passage from Deuteronomy 8, God is talking to the Israelites before they go into the Promised Land. He is reminding them of how He took care of them for forty years by not allowing their clothes and shoes to wear out. He reminds them of how He sent manna to feed them, not just to sustain and nourish their bodies, but also to train and test them so that they might learn to trust Him and obey His Word to them. In other words, He was saying, "I want you to learn to obey Me, because what I tell you to do is the right and best thing for you. I love you. Therefore, what I ask of you is for your own good."

God has not changed His mind. He is the same yesterday, today, and forever. God the Father told Jesus that He was His beloved Son in whom He was well pleased. Jesus was saying to the Devil, "I know I am the Son of God because my Father said so, not because I can turn stones to bread." It is important that the body of Christ see this truth.

The phrase, "that we live by every Word that proceeds from the mouth of God" has not been included in some translations of the Bible, such as the NIV. I believe that this omission has done a disservice to the people of God. Jesus most often quoted the Old Testament, and I am sure that in Luke's Gospel, He quoted all of Deuteronomy 8:3 to the Devil.

This question of identity is very important. The homosexual community believes one of the biggest lies ever told. Earl and I encountered a large population of gay men and women in the Midwest. They are a classic example of what I am trying to communicate within this section of the book.

While ministering to them, we discovered that almost all of them had an experience, or series of experiences, as a young child that gave them an identity with the homosexual community. They allowed the experience—not God—to give them an identity. As a youngster, for example, you may have stolen something. Did that give you a new identity as a thief? Many homosexuals say, "God made me this way; therefore, it's God's fault." That's a cop-out, a failure to take responsibility for their own actions and choices. It's tragic that we are seeing lives ruined in our culture because homosexuals believe the lie that God made them that way. Study the fifth chapter of Galatians, and read about the flesh and the spirit. This passage says that God made my flesh to enjoy sexual fulfillment, but I have to stop my flesh from doing whatever it wants to do.

After reading this book, if you want to send me mail to let me know I am homophobic, don't bother. Why is it so hard for the gay community to understand that we think their lifestyle is wrong? I have dealt with many different kinds of sin in my years of ministry: adultery, fornication, lying, thievery, and even murder. None of the people ever thought I did not like them because I said to them, "What you are doing is wrong because God says so."

Only the homosexual community cannot separate who they are from what they do. The real danger in our society today is that the culture is changing and their sinful behavior pattern is being redefined as just an alternative lifestyle. When the church agrees with this statement, there is no hope for the person caught in that lie. How dare the church leave them to their sin!

How do you see yourself? What is your identity? In what area are you not agreeing with God?

CHAPTER 45

TRUE SUCCESS

As I reflect back on the last fifteen years as the founding and senior pastor of Eagle's Nest Fellowship Church, I think the world would look on and say that I was successful, based on our membership, buildings, and other milestones. But those forms of measurement are really insignificant. True success is being in the center of God's will. I believe you will only be truly successful if you are where God wants you to be, doing what He has called you to do there.

The size of the sanctuary or the number of people who show up on Sunday morning may or may not be a sign of success. I remember being at a church in northwest Iowa that was really in the boondocks. To give you an idea of how much in the boonies this church was, the pastor's wife told us that it was ninety miles to the closest McDonald's.

About fifty people showed up for each service, and we really had church. The pastor and his wife were both Spirit-filled believers and knew that God had called them to this place. They were so happy, and it was contagious to everyone they met. They preached the Word and were experiencing revival when we got there. Though they may never make the cover of *Christianity Today*, these two servants of God are a tremendous success, ministering to about fifty people.

While I was writing this book, Mary Jane and I visited Calvary Chapel in Ft. Lauderdale. Pastor Bob Coy, the founding and senior pastor, started the church in 1985 after he moved from Las Vegas. We first visited Calvary Chapel in the year 2000 when they held their first service in their new worship center, which had once been an industrial complex. They basically fill this renovated facility that can seat about four thousand people four times every weekend. They average about twelve to fifteen thousand each weekend.

It's easy to feel inferior and less than successful when you come from a church that ministers to about eight hundred people weekly and visit a mega-church with a weekly attendance of fifteen thousand. But I once heard Pastor Coy say Calvary Chapel is ministering to only about one percent of the population in Greater Ft. Lauderdale. I later added up the attendance numbers at Eagle's Nest, along with the outreaches led by Pastor Rick and Pastor Carl, and I realized that we are also reaching about one percent of the population of our county.

Success, however, can't be exclusively measured with numbers, which affirmed me that we were being effective in reaching our community. There are many things we cannot offer that a mega-church does, yet there are also important similarities. The growth of both our churches has largely come from our emphasis on preaching the Word of God. The Bible, infused with the Holy Spirit, will change hearts and lives without any gimmicks. A strong emphasis on worship and praise, along with the teaching of the Word, must be the foundation of any successful church. We must make the Word relevant to our culture, but not at the expense of becoming part of the culture.

There is no magic formula for having a successful church, but I have noticed that the largest churches in America have at least four things in common:

1. They have been in their communities for several years, and they are committed to be there for the long haul. They have found favor in their communities through service and continuity.
2. They have a passion for the Word of God, knowing it has transforming power for those who read it, hear it, and believe it.
3. These churches love people, and they desire that no one should perish, but have everlasting life in Jesus.
4. They have a heart for praise and worship. You can have the most talented musicians and singers on the planet; but unless they are anointed to bring people into the presence of God, all you have is pretty music. There is a fine line between performance and ministry. Worship and praise is what brings us into His presence. The Psalmist had it right!

In Psalm 100:4, he exclaims, "Enter into His gates with thanksgiving and into His courts with praise." God does not have a complaint department. If you want God to hear you, begin to worship and praise Him.

Churches that are making disciples are using these four principles to grow in numbers, gifts, and God's grace, as well as to find favor in their communities.

CHAPTER 46

CALLED INTO MINISTRY

I said earlier that most churches mistakenly believe the pastor is supposed to do all the ministry, but it really is the pastor's job to train believers to do the work of ministry. I am often asked, "How does one know he or she is called into ministry?" Let me be blunt. If you are a born-again child of the Most High God and know that every sin is under the blood of Jesus Christ, then you are called into ministry (2 Corinthians 5:17-21)! You don't have to ask or pray about it. You are called by God and have been given the ministry of reconciliation as an ambassador for Christ.

How this occurs and becomes a reality for each of us may differ. I really believe that my call came in a very normal way, following the pattern of Isaiah's call to ministry that we find recorded in Isaiah 6. In these verses, Isaiah is sharing about his conversion, as well as his call to ministry. The sixth chapter begins with Isaiah giving the date and political scene of his day. The year

King Uzziah died, Isaiah found himself in the temple. (This is not a bad place to be if you are really hungering for God.) While in the temple—while in church, if you will—he saw the Lord.

I am convinced that all of us need to see the Lord! How? In my case I saw the Lord revealed through a group of people at a Lay Witness Mission. I did not physically see Jesus, but I saw evidence or fruit of Him revealed through this team. (Most of us feel pretty good about ourselves, at least I did. When I married Mary Jane, I cleaned up and even went to church. I looked good and was good. I wasn't saved, but I thought I was good.)

Then I saw Jesus in them. After I saw Jesus, I saw myself for the first time ever. After we see Jesus, we don't look so good anymore. We then have a choice. We will do one of two things: We will often hide out in church because this makes us feel better about ourselves, or we will do as Isaiah did when he cried out, "Woe is me, I am undone, I am a mess. I have unclean lips, and so do those around me."

I think he was saying, "I have seen my sin. I have seen God, and He will probably destroy me." The word "undone" can be translated as "destroy." But the good news of the gospel is when we cry out to the Lord, He will hear us; and He will always send an agent of change to make us brand new. In Isaiah's case it was a seraphim who brought a coal from the altar to touch him at the point of his sin and to cleanse it, or take it away.

CHAPTER 47

THE KEY

The key here is to cry out. To see your sin and not cry out just makes you more miserable. In my case, God sent a man, Earl Tyson, into our fellowship several months later to introduce me to the person and work of the Holy Spirit. When Earl laid hands on me at the altar, I have never felt so clean—inside and out. Only the Holy Spirit can do this. Let's re-examine the process:

1. We see God.
2. We see ourselves.
3. We cry out to God.
4. God cleanses us from our sin.
5. Now what?

Notice that throughout this whole process, God never asked Isaiah to go and do anything for Him. But now Isaiah hears the voice of God, which was (and still is) saying, "Who will go for me? Whom shall I send?" The "Now what?" at the end of the process is meant for the saints of God to step up and say, "Here I am, send me!"

CHAPTER 48

TEACHABLE AND AVAILABLE

On one occasion while traveling with Earl, I was missing home and feeling sorry for myself. I cried out to God, "Why me, when I would rather be home?" God answered me, "Two reasons. One, you didn't know anything, and two, you were available."

When God told me I didn't know anything, I think He was reminding me that because I didn't grow up in church, I didn't have a lot to "*un-learn*." I was teachable. I have discovered that it's hard to teach the Bible to people who already have their minds made up.

A lot of church people have heard Bible stories all their lives and think they have a handle on truth. I was teaching a Bible class years ago and asked the group how many of each kind of animals Noah took on the ark. Everyone in the class replied at once, "Two, a male and female of each kind."

They answered that way because in Sunday school they sang that Noah took them in by "two-sies, two-sies." That is a cute song for children, but it is poor theology. Genesis 7:2 says that "Noah should take seven each of every clean animal . . . and two each of animals that are unclean." The point is we have to study to show ourselves approved unto God, rightly dividing the Word of God.

The second reason God gave me was that I was available. I had told God, and meant it, that I would do whatever He asked me to do. Not once did I think about how unqualified I was. Most of us don't feel qualified, so we come up with excuses. When I was struggling to make my decision concerning going to Bible school or not, my major excuse that I gave to God was that I was forty-three years old and I would be forty-five after I spend two years in school. After one such session, it seemed as if God said to me, "Well, how old will you be in two years if you don't go?"

EXCUSES

When we make excuses, we are in good company. Remember Moses? When God told him he was going to use him to bring His people out of Egypt, Moses responded by asking, "Who am I?" I have tried to help you answer that question in this book. We all must discover whose and who we are before we can be of any use to God.

God's answer to Moses is the same one He gives us. He responded by saying, "I certainly will be with you." In other words, Moses will never be alone. He and God would make a majority. Jesus likewise said, "I will never leave you, nor forsake you." Once we go with God, we can expect to see the supernatural because the Supernatural One is with us all the time. Moses then asked God what His name was because the Egyptians would want to know. God said, "I Am Who I Am. Tell them that I Am has sent me to you." I love this name. Think of all the times Jesus said, "I Am." ("I Am The Way, The Truth, The Life, The Light, The Bread of Life," etc.) I don't know all that is contained here, but I know that He was saying to them, and is saying to us, "My name is not I was. I am not the God who was. Don't look for Me in the past: I am not there. My name is not I will be. Don't look for Me in the future. Don't be anxious for tomorrow. I am not there. I Am now. If you are regretting the past or anxious about the future, you are missing Me where I Am."

If you don't know for sure that God is "I Am," don't step out into ministry. But if you know this, then jump in with both feet and get started on the greatest ride of your life—the most exciting life you can imagine.

The next argument Moses used was, "What will I do if they won't listen to me?" I remember getting dressed one Sunday to go preach. About five hundred people were coming at this time, and I looked in the mirror and began to laugh. I was laughing because I couldn't believe that anyone would come to hear me say anything. Then God reminded me that they weren't coming to hear me.

Remember, when God is with you, it makes all the difference in the world. God asked Moses, "What do you have in your hand?" Moses had a rod. What do you have? Whatever it is, you need to let God cast the serpent out of it. The thing I held in my hand was my security of the past, wrapped up in some stock with Clyde Betts & Son. At the time, I thought I should keep hold of that stock, so if this ministry thing didn't work out I'd have that to fall back on. Now, I believe the one hundred and seventy acres the ministry owns today is the result of God casting out the serpent, but first I had to let go of what was in my hand.

The next excuse Moses used was that he could not talk; he was not eloquent of speech. God said to him and us, "I will be your mouth and teach you what to say." Then Moses got to the real issue. He plainly said, "Send someone else." I saw a book one time entitled *Here I Am, Lord: Send Aaron.* I think that describes a lot of us: "I don't want to get out of my comfort zone, so I hope God will send someone else."

I heard Calvary Chapel's Bob Coy tell his congregation that he wanted to let them in on a secret. He confessed that his church grew from a handful of believers in 1985 to fifteen thousand in 2007 because "Quite frankly, I don't know what I am doing."

I know that feeling! But Bob Coy knows God and that, my friend, is what prospers us as we live in obedience to His Word. I am convinced that there is great danger in thinking we are qualified to do anything for God. I believe Bob Coy and all other leaders in the body of Christ realize their dependency on God on a daily basis. Psalm 119:105 instructs us that God's Word is a lamp to our feet and a light to our path. There are many lessons in that verse, but the one I want to stress here is that God's Word to us usually does not include a five-year plan.

God's Word will give us enough light to take a few steps, but not enough to complete a five-year journey. As I have already said, if God had shown me the fifteen-year plan, I would have been too scared to even begin the journey. God loves us so much He does not want to scare us, but He does want to expand our faith by getting us to realize that we are not on this journey alone.

God not only has given us the Holy Spirit to live in us, but He also surrounds us with the Holy Spirit, also called the Helper or the Paraclete. He will lead and guide us, as well as enable us to do things far bigger than we could without Him. In the fall of 1991, when I heard the word from the Holy Spirit that the Saturday night Bible study should stop and we should continue to minister on Sunday mornings after Labor Day, I considered it strange. The Bible study had been held for about ten years and was very fruitful. When I announced that the services for the campers would continue after Labor Day, 1991, and that we would meet every Sunday, I never used the word "church." I just shared what I heard and sensed in my spirit—enough light to take the first step.

This is much like taking a fifty-mile trip in your car after dark and turning on the headlights, expecting to see down the road fifty miles. It does not work that way. Actually, we turn on the headlights and get about seventy-five to a hundred feet of light—one step if you will. But as we begin the journey, the light goes before us so that we continually get more light as we move. It's important to see that we only get more light as we move into the light we already have. If we stop, the light stops.

I believe most of us never begin to step out for God because we want to see the end when we begin. Don't wait. Begin to walk in what you have light for. Begin to obey what you have heard, and then you will begin to do extraordinary things for God.

On Easter Sunday 2000, a young lady who got saved would have an impact on others in a way I could not imagine. I would have to say that she was radically changed. After several months of living out her newfound faith, her Turkish-born Muslim husband came to a Wednesday night service and asked to see a pastor afterward. He pleaded with such emotion that those he talked with thought it was a demand. They were sure he wanted to argue or fight with someone. After they located Pastor Carl Vincent, the two men went into a classroom to talk. The Muslim husband stated, "My wife tells me she is a Christian. I don't know what happened to her, but I like it. I want Jesus to do it to me also!" Praise God!

About two or three years later, his Muslim parents from Turkey came for a visit. They stayed all summer and came to church every Sunday with their son's family, although they did not speak or understand a word of English. On the last Sunday before leaving to fly back to Turkey, they were in church again. After the message was preached, an invitation was given, and they asked their son if they could go forward. They said they had seen such a change in him because of the peace he had that they wanted God to do it to them also, and He did!

Since that time, both parents have gone to be with God in glory because of the changed life of their daughter-in-law. God knows no boundaries when it comes to language. The Holy Spirit can cut through any linguistic, racial, social and economic boundaries to make us all one and to bring us all unto Himself. Another reason this is so powerful is that the fruit of making a commitment to Christ is very visible to all. A commitment without change is not commitment at all. First the daughter-in-law came to Christ, then their son, then his mom and dad! This also is an example of the truth that what happens *to* you will happen *through* you. To God be the glory!

Eagle's Nest had a marvelous retirement party for Mary Jane and me in March 2007. One of the things that was such a blessing and brought back memories was a segment they called "This Is Your Life." People from our past were hiding behind a curtain, and we could only see their shadow. We were given clues, and we guessed their identities.

One man's clues brought back a profound memory. One morning I was driving to speak at a meeting in North Carolina and approaching the Chesapeake Bay Bridge Tunnel, about three hours from home. I began to sense an urgency to turn the car around and go home. As I continued to drive, the feeling just got stronger until I finally submitted and turned around to go home. Three hours later, I was almost home and trying to figure out what to say to the people who were expecting me to speak in North Carolina, since I had no idea why God had instructed me to turn around.

As I arrived at the crossover just north of our house in the middle of a driving rain, there sat a car. As I stopped, the driver got out in the rain and asked if he could follow me home and talk to me. After we were seated in my basement office, he said he had been to the campground, and they told him I was in North Carolina. I told him I was on my way there, but something told me to come back home.

He then began to tell me his story of depression, despair, and hopelessness. In a testimony he gave a year later, I found out for the first time that after he left the campground, and when I saw him in the crossover, he was on his way to take his own life. He had made all the plans as to where, when, and how. A mutual friend of ours had told him that morning to come see me because she could see how depressed he was, and he thought, "Why not?"

I spent about three or four hours with him, and God did the transformation. When he arrived home after that first visit, I received a phone call from his wife, whom I hadn't met. The conversation went something like this. "What in the name of God have you done to my husband?" After initially panicking, I thought, "Well, he was fine when he left here a little while ago . . ." I finally asked her, "What do you mean?"

She replied, "Well, he came in the house whistling a little while ago. I haven't heard him whistle in a year. What have you done to him?" I assured her that he was fine. He had just met Jesus in a profound way, and he would be different. This man is still walking with the Lord, and he told the crowd at my retirement dinner that I saved his life. In reality, it was the Lord who saved his life through this pig farmer who was learning to listen to Him.

This story also illustrates the truth of how God will use what happens to us to rescue others through us. A few months later, this same man stopped to visit a former co-worker who had left her employment because of health issues. When she saw him, she wanted to know what had happened to him because he looked so much better than he did the last time she had seen him. She said,

"You look so much better, at peace, and relaxed. What happened to you?"

He began to tell her his story of meeting Jesus and how that had changed him. As he shared, she began to weep and told him that when he pulled into her driveway, she was counting pills, trying to decide how many it would take to end her life. As this gentleman was relaying this incident to me later, he became quite excited and wanted to know if he did it OK. He said, "I just told her what you told me, and I tried to remember all the Scripture you gave me." Praise God! This is how it works: You only keep what you give away.

CHRISTIAN EDUCATION

The addition of the school was a natural transition from the daycare. Miss Lucy, as she is affectionately known, made the transition a smooth and natural process. Beginning with kindergarten, we added one class each year until we had eight grades. During this time we became part of a group of Christians who began to believe God for a Christian high school in the county seat of Sussex County: Georgetown. This became a reality when the high school opened in the fall of 2004.

My hope is that more churches in the county will begin K-8 grades and become feeder schools for Delmarva Christian High School. I thank God for Christian teachers in public schools, but I am convinced that Christian parents must provide Christian education for our children. A world view being taught in public schools today that must be changed says, "Either there is no God, or there are many gods. One is as 'good' or as 'bad' as the other."

As Christian parents, we can only change this when we take responsibility for our children's education. In one of his books, Rev. D. James Kennedy quoted the Puritan minister, Cotton Mather: "Religion begat prosperity, and the daughter has consumed the Mother. Because of our Christian heritage, America has achieved unparalleled success, but our success has caused us to forget God." I urge you to read Deuteronomy 8:10-18. Let me emphasize that Christian schools, Christian daycares, and even good churches cannot do what must be done in the home.

Parents, where are you in your walk with God? Do your children know your testimony? Do you have one? Do you instruct them in the "ways of God"? Do you say, "I am not qualified"? Then get into a Bible-believing, preaching church where the Word of God is taught, and get qualified!

After we began the campground, the church, the daycare, and then the school, we also knew God wanted us to start up other campuses around Kent and Sussex County. What is next? I truly don't know, but I don't feel like we have completed the "Call from the Cradle to the Grave."

Even though I officially retired in December of 2006, I would like to be a part of this vision, and I know that God will use me to make it a reality. I don't believe pastors and ministers should retire as long as they are able to minister to other people. I also know that when God gives the vision, He supplies the people with skills and gifts we do not have. As our ministry grew, it was obvious that we needed help in the area of details. I am a visionary, but not good with details. (This may work for a while, but not as you get larger and larger.) In the midst of our need, God sent Lucy Dutton, Sonny Reed, Bob Weed and many others to work for God's vision He had given to us. Habakkuk says, "Write the vision that people may run to help with the vision." This is how the Kingdom works.

This is important, especially for those of you reading this who may be in a position of authority. Find staff members who have a love for God and people, but who also can and will embrace the vision of the senior pastor. A body with more than one head is a freak. Bob did what was asked of him and did it well. Bob is now the lead pastor at Eagle's Nest, and I am convinced that he will move the church into the next level with wisdom, grace, and godly leadership. No senior pastor can do it all alone, even if you are a small congregation. They may not be paid staff, but you need Ephesians 4 people to surround you with gifts and abilities you don't have.

I want to conclude this book with some practical instructions on how to get out of the pigpen. There is nothing wrong with being in the pigpen if you are where God wants you to be. The pigpen for this book just represents where you are now. Where are you spiritually? Are you restless? Are you unfulfilled, feeling like you want to do something for God, but don't know what? Let me share with you some things I have learned.

The number-one thing is to start where you are, with what you have. I am certain that we don't build ministries; God gives us ministries.

In the early days of Eagle's Nest Fellowship Church I did a lot of marriage ministry. I did not ask for, look for, feel qualified for, or seek in any way all the people who found their way to my door. God sent them. I have discovered that ministry flows from overflow. Fruit is excess life. You give away out of the overflow, or you end up depleting your own life.

The very first couple I ministered to was a friend whom I went to see the first day after getting home from Bible school in 1981. When I walked into his place of business, he rushed over to talk and told me that his wife had moved out three days earlier. He asked if I would go and see her. I never felt so helpless in my life. Because I cared, I said yes and went to see her. God did the rest. They are still married and very happy more than twenty-seven years later. To God be the glory! Proof came again that God will use whoever will go, not just the qualified.

The second thing you must have is a desire to help people. Every good leader must be a servant. Our example is Jesus Himself. Think about this. In John 13, after spending three years with His disciples teaching them by word and example, He is preparing them for His departure and wants to sum up all He has been saying to them for three years. So, He has a meal with them, and after dinner He girds Himself with a towel and begins to wash their feet.

He then gives them a challenge, "Go and do the same." The message is clear. If you want to be used of God, become a foot-washer. That means do whatever needs to be done to help hurting people. I really think my passion began back in the early eighties while we were visiting the PTL Club in South Carolina during the golden years of Jim and Tammy Faye Bakker.

The guest that night was singer/songwriter, Mike Murdock, who wrote many of the songs Tammy Faye sang. He sat at the piano and sang a song that somehow touched my heart in a special way. The chorus of that song goes like this, "I want to spend my life mending broken people/I want to spend my life removing pain/Lord, let my words heal a heart that hurts/I want to spend my life mending broken people."

I found myself weeping and saying, "So do I Lord, so do I."

If that is your heart, join me and jump into the Kingdom life and get involved! God may not lead you to the pulpit from your personal pigpen, but He will definitely lead you to where you are supposed to be, doing what it is He wants you to do. And trust me, there is no better place to be in this world.

ABOUT THE AUTHOR

Bill Sammons was born in 1937, the second of three sons to Andrew and Anna Sammons in Milton, Delaware. His parents instilled the American work ethic in Bill, and he became a successful farm manager and salesman for a local agricultural enterprise. But in 1980, at 43 years of age, he left the farm and his family to begin a new phase in his life. Little did he know what the future would hold. Today, Bill is the retired founding pastor of one of Delaware's largest ministries, which includes a church, daycare, Christian school, public campground, and soon, a radio station. Bill and his wife Mary Jane still live in Milton, where he grew up and graduated from high school, near where they raised their only son, Bill Jr., and where they enjoy their family, including three grandchildren and two great grandchildren. It's been many years since Bill was in the pigpen, and he still frequents the pulpit anytime he is invited.

Bill and Mary Jane Sammons
Photo by Steve Theis

ORDER THE BOOK

Send a check for $20 per book
+ $5 Shipping & Handling
payable to:

William T. Sammons
12984 Coastal Highway
Milton, DE 19968

(302) 684-5453 • (302) 381-2511

Fruitbearer Publishing
P. O. Box 777, Georgetown, DE 19947
(302) 856-6649 • FAX (302) 856-7742
www.fruitbearer.com
Email: info@fruitbearer.com